CHAMBERS FOR A MEMORY PALACE

THE TOWER OF BEQUIA

A MEMORY PALACE

by
or

d

pore :

ndence,
llard.

94-33012
CIP

HARLES W. MOORE
Y THE AUTHORS

s s
HUSETTS
ND

This book was set in Bembo by DEKR Corporation and was printed an
bound in the United States of America.

Library of Congress Cataloging-in-Publication Data

Lyndon, Donlyn.
  Chambers for a memory palace / Donlyn Lyndon and Charles W. M₁
  with illustrations by the authors.
    p. cm.
  Includes index.
  ISBN 0-262-12182-4
  1. Lyndon, Donlyn—Correspondence. 2. Moore, Charles Willard,
1925-   —Correspondence. 3. Architects—United States—Corresp₁
4. Architecture—Composition, proportion, etc. I. Moore, Charles W
1925–   . II. Title.
NA737.L96A3 1994
720—dc20

CONTENTS

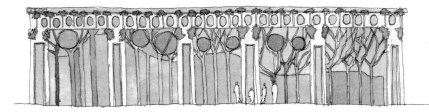

ACKNOWLEDGMENTS

Several people deserve special thanks for their help in the preparation of this book. Kevin Keim and Terezia Nemeth have each helped in many ways, assembling material, proffering valuable advice, and generally helping to keep the enterprise afloat (and well fed). A companion throughout, Alice Wingwall has lent a generous and discriminating ear to our discussions and text as well as providing some deft phrases. Jacquelyn Baas offered frequent encouragement and an occasional jump start on descriptions. Our offices—Moore/Andersson in Austin and Lyndon/Buchanan in Berkeley—provided continuous logistical support, most especially from Barbara Shepherd, Chris Fenner, Melisa Nelson, and Susi Marzuola. We are indebted to Allan Jacobs for a close reading of the text and grateful for Melissa Vaughn's sympathetic precision in editing.

Charles Moore did not live to see this book in print, though the manuscript and illustrations were complete. It was the focus of time we spent together during the last several years (in the Castello di Gargonza, Siena, Berkeley, Austin, and The Sea Ranch), and it is the repository of nearly forty years of friendship and discussion. I will always be grateful for that special palace of memories.

Donlyn Lyndon
The Sea Ranch, California
January 1994

INTRODUCTION

The Idea of Place and a Place for Ideas

Two thousand years ago Marcus Tullius Cicero used to make two-hour speeches in the Roman Senate, without notes, by constructing in his mind a palace whose rooms and furnishings, as he imagined himself roaming through them, called up the ideas he wished to discuss: ideas were made memorable by locating them in space.

Cicero, we would like to think, lived in a world (or at least could imagine one) in which space and structure had a clear and recognizable order. Traditions governing the organization of rooms and building parts allowed them to be related to each other, yet they were sufficiently differentiated so that they could serve as reminders of events and experiences that took place within them. You could tell one space from another either by its position in a larger pattern or by its distinctive shape or characterizing detail. It's all rather startlingly like the "architecture" of computers, with information stored by location and accessed by a system of coordinates (or by a mouse darting around on the screen, nibbling at images positioned in boxes).

The architectures of places then made it possible to think about them with some subtlety and to ally particular ideas and events with specific forms and shapes and their relationships. Places could bring emotions, recollections, people, and even ideas to mind; their qualities were a part of a culture's intellectual equipment.

What Cicero was able to take for granted we must at this point discover. The scope of change in our everyday environments has outpaced the accumulation of wisdom and craft that traditionally guided the making of places; indeed, much of what was previously known has in haste been set aside, leaving a blank slate. Worse yet, there are those who would abandon the tangible world altogether in favor of a virtual reality assembled in computer networks—Memory Palaces dislodged from the earth and inhabited by electronic speculations. We intend to remain unabashedly earthbound, ready to spend our limited days imagining palpable places, places that people can reach on their feet and fill with their presence.

Places are spaces that you can remember, that you can care about and make a part of your life. Much of what is built now is too tepid to be remembered. The spaces with which we are surrounded are so seldom memorable that they mean little to us. We think it should be otherwise, that the world should be filled with places so vivid and distinct that they can carry significance.

Places that are memorable are necessary to the good conduct of our lives; we need to think about where we are and what is unique and special about our surroundings so that we can better understand ourselves and how we relate to others. This mental intermingling of people, places, and ideas is what makes architecture interesting.

Our purpose in writing this book is to help make real places more memorable; to inscribe some suggestions for building that will make the actual world of buildings and landscapes capable of carrying ideas for those who live among them—

rendering them as valuable to thought as Cicero's imaginary palaces were to speech.

In the following pages we assemble a set of observations on the composition of places. We cast these observations as Chambers for a Memory Palace, each with a title. The titles consist of elements (nouns) and actions (verbs). The elements are ones that we have found to be present in architecture throughout the world; the actions describe how these elements shape the experiences that a place affords. We think that architecture must be considered this way: that it is made up of nameable parts as well as ephemeral sensations, and that these parts work together to affect how we live in places and what they bring to mind. The nouns in themselves are of little significance; it is the way they act to structure our experiences that affects us.

Each of the Chambers we have named has a diagram and a simple descriptive statement. Each may be imagined as an empty room—a space to be inhabited with memories of real places. To bring these Chambers to life we have written letters to each other, recollecting examples of buildings and landscapes that incorporate the elements and actions we've named. Our letters are not meant to fill the Chambers, but to stage a sort of housewarming. We hope that readers will more fully populate them with their own observations.

In calling these Chambers for a Memory Palace, we insist on their flexibility. They are categories of convenience, meant to help assemble thoughts about places. The Chambers are not intended to limit or confine, but rather to nurture sparks in the designer's consciousness. These Memory Chambers then are starting points, aids to the imagination, not recipes for design. With them you can enliven the arduous and joyful task of making places—nooks, rooms, buildings, gardens, landscapes, and cities in which spirits can play and the mind can build a Palace.

As treatises on geometry develop from point to line to surface to solid, the Themes in our set of Memory Chambers might start with a line—an axis (if it is straight) or a path (if it wanders), then proceed to orchards that multiply the lines onto a plane, and then to platforms, slopes, and stairs that raise some of the places into the third dimension. After that, we can enclose our spaces with walls and borders pierced with doors and windows and sheltering pockets of space at the edge, cover our space with roofs and canopies, stud it with markers, and then have a look at how we animate it with light and ornament. The rooms we assemble in Compositions can draw on recollections and expectations or embody a nebulous sense of order. They will surely include gardens and be blessed by the magic of water. To test the assembled observations, we return in a postscript to a single place, the Castello di Gargonza, to see how this humble fortified village in Tuscany would fit into the Chambers of our Palace. Simple buildings, as well as grand ones, are meant to fit there.

● THEMES

Vaux-le-Vicomte, France

1 AXES THAT REACH / PATHS THAT WANDER

THEMES   *Axes that Reach / Paths that Wander*

Axes reach across space to draw together the important points in a place. They are mental constructs that help us to position ourselves and make alliance with things, buildings, or spaces. Paths are where your feet actually trod, so that what happens along the way becomes the important thing. In some of the most interesting places, axes and paths interweave, with the axis allowing the mind to do the connecting, and the path allowing the feet to wander, explore, make choices, and put things in sequence.

DEAR CHARLES, Axes are, after all an extension of being face to face; when you want to be certain to give your full attention to someone, or to signal that you are doing so, you position yourself opposite them, your bodies roughly aligned, your eyes attending to theirs. Likewise with objects: when we really want to pay close attention, we tend to place our whole bodies before them. Purveyors of religion learned this at the very beginning, and the history of religious architecture is characterized by forms and spaces organized along axes that extend the reach of several objects or chambers through long halls, courts, and forecourts to the outer limits of the sacred precinct. The builders of secular spaces, too, recognized the organizational power of the axis and arranged palaces and civic spaces along lines that lead through entire complexes, even cities, marshalling the attention of all those in attendance, separating left from right and setting the stage for processions.

The axis Eliel Saarinen drew across what must once have been a loose terrain behind the backyard of his house at the Cranbrook Academy of Art probably didn't cost him a great lot of intellectual energy. Once it was determined that there should be a museum and library of some considerable pretension on the rise of ground near the Cranbrook swimming hole, it must have been a fairly obvious device. This would be especially so on the grounds of the complexes he designed earlier for the Boy's School and the Academy. An observer moving through these spaces is almost always aligned with something:

an arch, a gate, an entry, a playing field. Even the street
Saarinen lived on ends in that fat and jolly sculpture of Jonah
and the Whale splattering water all over a terrace that overlooks
the swimming hole.

But what a difference that new axis to the museum and
library makes. How much more splendor it lends to the occasion. It reaches from the street right through the buildings and
beyond to a grove of trees, with the uplifted faces of Carl
Milles's ring of sculptures becoming ecstatic as it passes among
them. This axis befuddles conventional wisdom because it leads
to a space, not an object. Saarinen knew perfectly well that
most people have been led to expect that following an axis leads
finally to being face to face with a building and its entrance (or
a tomb, or the king's bedroom at Versailles). This path, marked

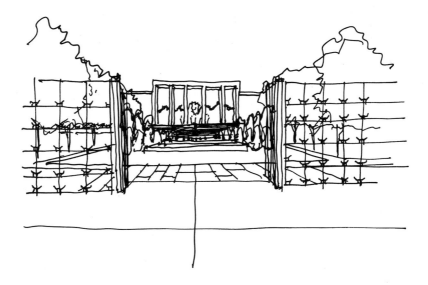

Cranbrook Academy of Art, Bloomfield Hills, Michigan

through space by ponds, statues, trees, sculpture, and steps, leads to a question—to a tall portico open to gardens on both faces and with entrances to the library and the museum on either side. The climax of the axis is a choice, not an instruction; enter the library to read, enter the museum to view, pass on to the grounds beyond, or linger. Saarinen obviously meant for some to linger and explore—why else the occasional raised meander on the sandstone piers, or for that matter the ring of more-than-life-size figures that Milles has caused to float in the spray of the fountain? And for those who are prone to a reflection more cerebral than that provided by those pools leading up to the colonnade, there's the evocatively sculpted "Europa and the Bull" standing ready to bring forth mythic speculation.

But this description is too diagrammatic—implying, as all too many would assume, that in making an axis, one simply sets up a line down which people can walk. This is not the case at all. An axis is a relationship across space, not simply a path. At best it is a thing of the mind, not just of the feet. In this case Saarinen drew a relationship between openwork metal gates at the public street (point of access from metropolitan Detroit) to the entry loggia set within the grounds of the Academy. Most of the area directly on the axis is given over to a stepped set of pools with paths on either side that reach up in gentle stages to broad stairs that stretch across the width of the loggia. The visitor's sequence is as follows: glimpse the axis when driving by (the relationship is very clear, an invitation has been extended); approach through the gates directly on axis (when they are open—the invitation has limits); move to the right or left around the pools and stroll along their edges (these are bordered

Cranbrook Academy of Art, Bloomfield Hills, Michigan

by flat ledges and planting); ascend slightly, a few steps at a time, as the levels of the pools rise (with bronze fish and game sporting in their midst); pass by Europa teasing the Bull's tongue at the head of the uppermost pool and angle across the broad steps (these rise in groups of ten or so at a time, with landings in between); arrive at the loggia and prepare to make your choice.

  The whole sequence is much simpler than many others, of course. Take, for instance, the axis that connects the entry portal of the Taj Mahal gardens in Agra, India, with the domed tomb itself. There the actual path plays back and forth along the axis in three dimensions. Within a geometrically simple walled apparition of a paradise garden, the path takes the observer through a measured set of experiences. When you first approach the great red sandstone gatehouse, you are funnelled to its center by flanking walls and a tall arch. As you enter this canopied space your attention is drawn to a glimmering vision that fills the space of the arch on the other side, a white dome whose profile matches that of the arch and whose base and entrance are directly ahead on the same level, but hundreds of paces away. Through the arch on axis with that domed tomb, the ground falls away into an expanse of bordered gardens with stone walks, flower beds, and ornamental trees spreading before you. Instinctively you step over to the side on the entry terrace and pause to absorb the literally breathtaking scene. To proceed, however, you must return to the central axis, as though to pay homage to the tomb, for the steps down off this broad terrace are barely a few paces wide and directly on the axis.

Taj Mahal, Agra, India

You soon reach the end of a long reflecting pool and, as at Cranbrook, move to the right or the left to parallel the pool. The axis continues through the center of the pool, marked by a row of white marble blossom shapes alternately emitting bubbling jets and plumes of fine spray to vary the reflections. Midway to the shining tomb your path is interrupted by a raised platform and cross-axial pools. Here you must return again to the main axis, where a narrow set of steps climb up onto what is effectively a

Taj Mahal, Agra, India

Taj Mahal, Agra, India

stage in the middle of the garden. But at center stage there is a flower-shaped pool; it is not your show. To continue toward the dome you must move around the periphery to the opposite side, to the axis again and down an identically narrow stair to the side of a pool, twin to the first, that reaches to the base of the tomb. There, as the pool ends, paths move back again to the center where a broad set of steps narrows as it ascends on axis to the white marble and red sandstone platform on which sits the base of the tomb. Now, however, the dome is out of sight. The tall, white, blank wall of the base fills your vision; an unexpected end to a ritually choreographed approach.

To reach the tomb itself (if you are allowed—and presumably not everyone was), you must move to the left or right along the base until you find one of the openings on either side that doubles back into the wall. There you ascend a steep set of stairs at right angles to the axis, your view centered on one of the minarets that help stake out the four corners of the tomb base. Once on the top, in a gleaming world of white marble, you turn back toward the central axis and move diagonally to a door filled with black shadow. This is the same door with which you were strictly aligned when you first saw the white domed apparition from the gatehouse. Here, isolated by the great square platform raised above the garden, everything is black and white, mostly dazzling white, with flowers carved in the marble walls with exquisite delicacy—a garden of frozen delight, made more chilling by the living garden below. Inside under the dome at the terminal point of the axis is a white marble cenotaph marking the position of Mumtaz Mahal's body below—as bereft of the quickness of life as the elegantly formed, pure, white, enduring stone that surrounds it.

In this monument the perfection that Shah Jahan wished to associate with his wife's memory required a balance of elements all around: the central dome is accompanied by lesser cupolas and framed by four minarets at the corners of the base. The symmetrical four-square approach garden with axial reflecting pools is on one side, the river flows crosswise on the other. A red sandstone domed mosque across the platform to the east is balanced by a mirror-image structure sheltering

Taj Mahal, entry gate, Agra, India

empty space at the opposite end on the west, each centered on the tomb's cross axis. With the resources and authority available to a cultured sixteenth-century despot, nothing was to be left undetermined. If you had chosen at the beginning of your path to fork left around the pool rather than right, your approach to the tomb would have been no different.

At Cranbrook, however, that choice does make a difference. The axis creates a broad artful passage that mediates between the elegantly contrived neatness of the domestically scaled residences and studios of the Academy on the left and a small valley that moves off diagonally behind trees to the right, the latter an only slightly tamed version of the unruly rolling landscape that preceded the Academy's presence here. Saarinen leaves room for understanding the world in multiple ways.

● DEAR DONLYN, I'm glad you included the two very different attitudes toward axes at Cranbrook and the Taj Mahal. The cross axis, or minor axis perpendicular to the major one, is worth some special attention, I think. One of particular historical moment is at Vaux-le-Vicomte, southeast of Paris, where according to the story, young Andre le Nôtre broke the boundaries of previous garden planning by inserting a cross-axial canal (out along the major axis) that burst out of the confines of the garden, out of sight to the right and left, into the wild woods, into which previous gardens had never stepped. Le Nôtre was then taken away in 1662 to design the gardens for

Vaux-le-Vicomte, France

Vaux-le-Vicomte, France

the Sun King at Versailles, where he achieved a main axis without end, stretching into the infinite; but the first break had come at Vaux-le-Vicomte.

The baroque world was filled with axial vistas to infinity in cities like Karlsruhe in Germany. L'Enfant overlaid them on his grid for Washington, D.C., as Sixtus V had carved

Versailles, France

Closed axis (after Camillo Sitte)

them through the tangle of medieval Rome. L'Enfant's diagonal streets and circles turn out, on inspection, to be thoughtfully sited for the long views, with the circular intersections located, where possible, at the tops of hills. Nearly a century later Camillo Sitte was to write a treatise against infinite expanses in his *Art of Building Cities,* to urge that an axis would end in a solid, to make, in a more medieval way, a strong sense of enclosure, and no infinities. It's an axis either way; the difference is in what you reach for.

I've been working on an axis at the Beverly Hills Civic Center in California that is quite different from either Cranbrook or the Taj Mahal, or even from the cross-axial Vaux-le-Vicomte. Here, where a series of civic buildings, existing and proposed, were in desperate need of a device that would link them to the larger landscape, I chose an axis, the longest the site afforded (running southwest to northeast), not located so that it

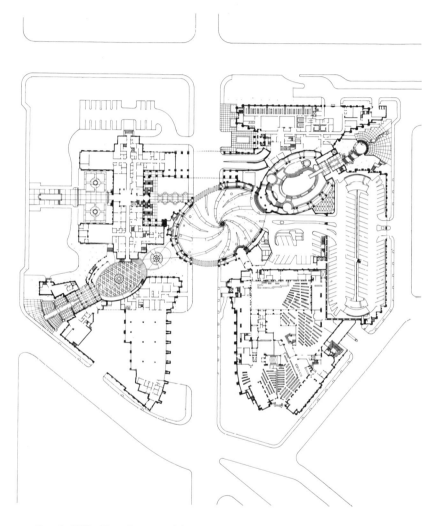

19

Beverly Hills Civic Center, California

would ever be traversed end-to-end, or even for a major part of its length. The axis is formed like a string of beads—each bead an elliptical open space, which can be read just for itself, or for the whole axial string.

The Beverly Hills axis, meant more to give a direction for the imagination to move, to structure the numerous pieces of the site, than for the feet to trod, has nonetheless a kind of urgency and force we associate with the axis. Quite opposite is the wandering path, the invitation to linger, to hesitate, even to choose between alternatives. I have taken to asking my students each year to read Jorge Luis Borges's "The Garden of Forking Paths," which I mention with some hesitation, because I don't want to lose the story's impact by giving away the plot, but the possibility of a place that takes its shapes to suit alternate realities seems to belong in our world.

The most ubiquitous figure to accommodate alternate realities, the most evenhanded and perhaps democratic, is of course the grid. It surfaced in Hellenistic Greece (as in Miletus), was later mandated by the Laws of the Indies for the colonies of sixteenth-century Spain (as in Puebla), and was much on Thomas Jefferson's mind when the settlement of the American northwest territories was being planned early in the nineteenth century. The most evident reason for the popularity of the grid system is the ease of administration and convenient sale of properties of roughly equal values. (When Austin, Texas, was plotted in 1836, lots were put on sale for $5; $10 on the main street, Congress Avenue. When the lots didn't sell well, a subsequent sale date was organized, with the same unobjectionable prices.)

The grid, granted, is made up of straight lines as are axes, with no suggestion of languor or hesitancy, though with

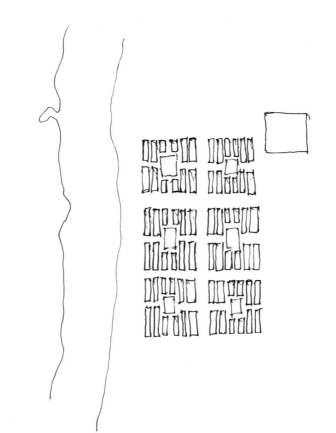

Savannah, Georgia

maximum built-in alternatives, and some special grids weight the unweighted choices: a notable American variant is the grid Lord Oglethorpe devised for Savannah, Georgia, based on an ideal city of the Italian Renaissance. Here each neighborhood benefits from a green square. The streets that run north-south between squares and around each have the advantage of a broken traffic-way, discouraging fast through traffic. The

21

north-south streets that run between these go straight through
and have no special advantage; they have collected the suppor-
tive businesses and services and suffer from fast traffic. The east-
west streets, though, have maintained a bonus value, since the
sides of the squares impart extra value not only to the buildings
facing the square but to the ones beside them, so that houses
not directly on the square share the benefits bestowed on their
neighbors. The east-west streets not bordering the squares are
boulevarded, so they are advantaged as well and have maintained their values. We don't know how much of this enhance-
ment value was predicted by Lord Oglethorpe, but by now we
can accurately measure the success of this weighted grid in
terms, anyhow, of the livability of this design for a city.

     If a grid, or the development of it, is a kind of anti-
axis, a substitution of the many for the one, then another
equally dramatic opposite to the axis is the wandering path. The
path can serve just the feet, while the mind darts along an axis.
Or, the wandering path can be the way for both the feet and
the mind to travel. Among the most striking paths are in stroll
gardens, usually around a Japanese or an English lake. At their
richest, these are organized like a narrative. The path around
the lake at Stourhead, England, filled with a richness of detail,
was designed to tell a story familiar to the eighteenth-century
connoisseur circumambulating the garden: the story of Aeneas
on his way to Rome. Changes in tempo are characteristic of
such a story, with carefully choreographed indirection, a wandering path whose narrative is measured in time. Not everybody,
then or now, knew the story of Aeneas, but the detail and the
pace of its introduction strike a rhythm more complex than
most any geometry.

Some wandering paths tell a story untranslated, which builds its richness and its subtlety on the garden materials alone. In two stroll gardens in Tokyo, Rikugi-en and Koraku-en, the format is similar to Stourhead: a path goes around a small lake with islands, sometimes at the very shore, sometimes up a slope. Here the paths that wander among clusters of precisely scaled foliage, with sequences of opening and closing vistas and alternating tree cover and open sky, are under complete control, determined by subtle geometries: an experiential tale with exquisite timing.

A building type especially beholden to an understanding of Axes that Reach and Paths that Wander is the museum, which people move through purposefully or casually, some intent on arriving at an anticipated goal, others

Stourhead, England

wandering, enjoying the pleasures along the way. As a visitor to a museum, you want to be able to lose yourself in exploration, but you also want to know where you are at any moment. Successful museums allowed either mode. The Uffizi in Florence is built along both sides of a short but important street that connects the city's main square with a walk along the river. Though it was built first to house government offices, it works splendidly as a museum. The axial street suggests purposeful motion in the city, while the galleries, in a variety of sizes and shapes, set up local rhythms, places to tarry—to look, say, at the Botticellis—without being, ever, beyond the call of the larger axial organization.

A museum with an organizational idea separate from the city, looking to somewhere else, is the Isabella Stewart Gardner in Boston, set in a palace around a cortile redolent of Venice. The great covered courtyard, exotic in the northern city, provides at once the image of the place and the key to circulation during a visit: around the edge is a ring of galleries, all of them different yet inexorably linked, so as to form a kind of circumferential axis, a version of the straight but looped around the garden; recognizable alternatively as a wandering path, where the major interest is in the incident, the alcove, the bay, or the group of furnishings.

The Louisiana Museum, on a beautiful stretch of woodland near the sea not far from Copenhagen, is most purely of all a path that wanders. It draws the viewer along via a richly variegated but never random pattern, always specific to the character of the space, the view of a particular corner of the woods or

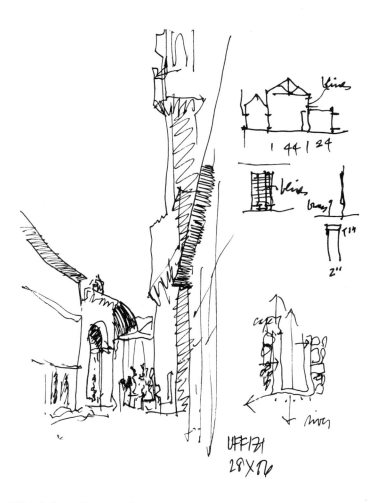

Uffizi Gallery, Florence, Italy

some special rocks or plants, never repeating, always gently leading the viewer forward, at his own speed, in an experience with
its own rhythms gently held together on its own time.

A fourth museum, the Kimbell in Fort Worth, Texas, designed by Louis Kahn, perhaps most effectively of all combines two opposites. There is a regularity to the order of construction that gives a repeating, even inexorable rhythm based on multiple elongated concrete vaults, each with its own axis lodged in the space above our heads, but the clarifying suggestion of directed motion these make is lifted off the floor, leaving an astonishing freedom for paths to wander among a wide variety of objects, paintings, and sculpture, bathed in filtered

Louisiana Museum, Denmark

light. The bright Texas sunlight is reflected away from the art-
works and similarly allowed to roam free over the underside
of the concrete vaults. The whole is remarkably free, never
hemmed in; the clear order of construction and support, with
each piece reaching to the next in parallel rows, serves more as
an inspiration than a guide. Here the rigor of Axes that Reach
is in almost perfect balance with the freedom of Paths that
Wander.

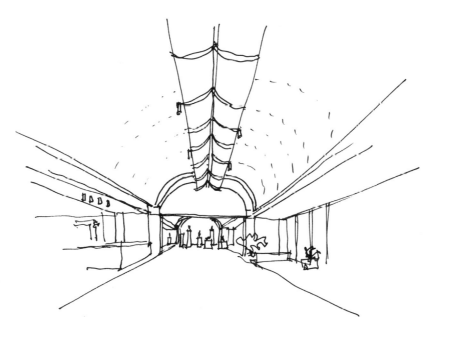

Kimbell Art Museum, Texas

Park project, Indianapolis, Indiana

Orderly rows of trees, columns, or piers mark off modules in a field of space. In architecture as in orchards, the intervals between uprights make a measure you can count and count on. The rhythmic measure that columns make in space so satisfies that it is often imprinted on the surface of buildings by pilasters that temper our perceptions.

D E A R   D O N L Y N ,   As the first chamber of our Memory Palace of architectural elements involves axes—points along a line—it seems appropriate that the second chamber deal in a grid of points on a plane that extend upward to make an orchard of orderly rows of trees or columns or piers to mark off modules in a field of space, and establish a rhythmic order that pulls us in. The most vivid examples are usually orchards themselves, where regular intervals of trees make, as we move by, arcades between the trees ahead of us as well as diagonally to the right and left—superimposed and even ambiguous orderings from the same grid.

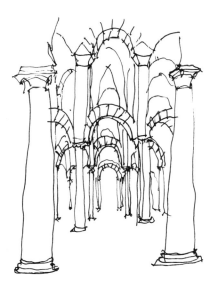

Great Mosque at Córdoba, Spain

The building in all the world that has the most magical orchardness is, for me, the Great Mosque at Córdoba. Forty years later I remember still the moment when I arrived at its door, which was open and admitted enough light into the shadowy interior for me to discern the first rows of columns marching into the darkness beyond. It was my first

glimpse of Islam, of an order of rhythm, not of hierarchy—
sufficiently muddled, as it turned out, by the Christian interposi-
tion of a cathedral into the vastness, and by older walls that
defined the realm of one Abd-er-Rahman from the next. Years
later, I finally saw the mosque at Kairouan in Tunisia where a
similar format is purer and simpler, an undefiled product of a
single building program, an uninterrupted orchard of columns.
It was a great disappointment, all too clear.

I suppose the memory of the thrill of peering into the
shadows of that mutilated masterpiece at Córdoba (unfocused
except for the uniqueness of some of the special vaults and the
burly Christian interventions) prompted my proposal at an exhibition for an orchard that measures—a grid of cardboard columns evenly spread, and held at the top by an arboreal tangle of
plywood moose antlers, but separately patterned in homage to
Domènech y Montaner's Catalan Music School in Barcelona,
though his are tile and mine are only paint.

It is worth noting that the notion of orchards has many
variations in plan, with a square grid possible, or a rectangular
grid, or one of equilateral triangles, a quincunx, which is the
most effective packing of trees as well. The quincunx was even
given, in the seventeenth century, mystical powers as a revela-
tion of "the mystical mathematics of the City of Heaven."

Three orchards in the courtyards of what were mosques
might go into this Memory Chamber. At Córdoba, the courtyard in front of the mosque has two grids in plan. One is a grid
of orange trees with a pattern of stone-lined irrigation channels
leading water to them. Overlaid on the orange trees there is a
larger grid of palms, which float free in the stone terrace, be-

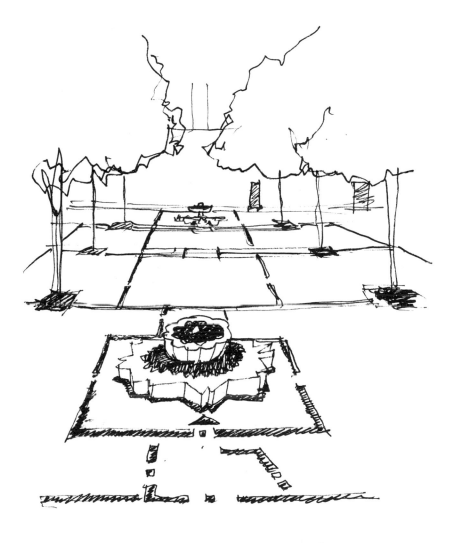

35

Sirille

Patio of the Orange Trees, Seville, Spain

cause the palms don't need irrigation to their roots. At Seville,
in the Patio of the Orange Trees in the courtyard of the cathedral (once the courtyard of the mosque), the three-dimensional
pattern of the orchard is reinforced in the brick paving. It is
paved in brick with channels from fountains to the bases of the
trees. Frequent bridges over the channels, each made with a simple brick, cause the brick surface to seem more continuous,
help it survive the erosion of the web of channels, and force the
plane of the water back down into the shiny cove of the crev-
ices. Then, far more simply, in the courtyard of the Koutoubia
in Marrakesh the surface is dirt and the channels that bring
water to the grid of the orange trees are made with little ridges
of dirt. The channels, once again, reinforce the orchard grid
that modulates the plane.

● DEAR CHARLES, Orchards of stone should certainly
make up a large part of our collection. In south India there are
many thousand-pillared *mandapas* that, like the mosque at Córdoba, extend almost out of sight into the darkness. Generally
these are each the result of a single building campaign, but un-
like the mosque at Kairouan they are imbued with subtle variations that establish a hierarchy of position inside. The central
aisle may be wider, for instance, and its columns most likely
carved in more complicated patterns. The rows to either side
may be raised slightly, set on platforms that make them places
of rest, storage, or gathering rather than passages. Or the stone
slabs that span between them may be more ornately carved.

Thousand-pillared mandapa, *Madurai, India*

Sometimes a stone slab will be raised slightly to let in a trickle of light and to allow ventilation. In any case, the experience of being in one of these apparently endless fields of columns will be varied as you penetrate into the darkness from the edge, which is usually open to allow breezes to sweep through these shaded passages. In these places you know your position in the gridded field by the amount of light, the sculpted iconography of the columns, and the nature of the surfaces overhead and underfoot. The great lobby of tall columns in Le Corbusier's Assembly Hall at Chandigarh is a recent variant on this archetype—minus the mythic carvings.

In Western architecture the orchard is seldom so explicit, but the measured bay marked out upon the ground and

Santo Spirito, Florence, Italy

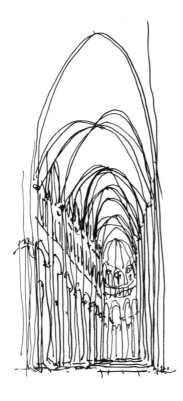

Bourges Cathedral, France

built up into space as columnar uprights, with members spanning between, is recurrent. The regularly paced aisles of Gothic churches come closest to the orchard motif, with their ribs branching into vaults overhead. In Bourges Cathedral, the tall, double side aisles on either side of the nave cause the space to spread generously and mysteriously, as under the branches of a wondrously tall orchard. Beech trees in Normandy send branches out into space as tendons that look astonishingly like the articulated ribs of Rouen Cathedral. However, the most literally treelike webs of ribbing are found in the hall churches of Germany, Poland, and Czechoslovakia. These churches, where all the piers are at the same height, create uniform fields of space that are often built with vaults traced by networks of ribbing that spring without interruption from those piers, creating an arboreal cover for the congregation below.

Hall churches, however, are an exception. Most large buildings that are given measure by a grid of columns have aisles of differing widths and heights with an obvious hierarchy

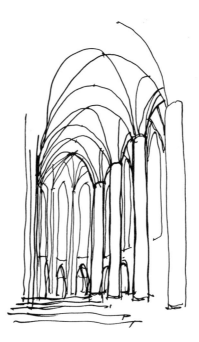

Church of the Jacobins, Toulouse, France

of positions—central nave and aisles to either side in most churches, for instance. These can have a radiant clarity of modulation. For ease of imagery we have used the orchard grid as the emblem of a system of bay spacings that mark out positions in space. The uniformity it implies is readily imagined. However, the fundamental proposition is prone to great variation. Spatial rhythms marked out by columns or piers and covered, often, by vaults or coffered ceilings occur throughout the history of architecture in a range of differing intervals and combinations that is potentially nearly as great as the variations on a simple rhythmic beat that characterize the world of music—though the practical benefits of ordering materials in repetitive sizes has tended to diminish the range.

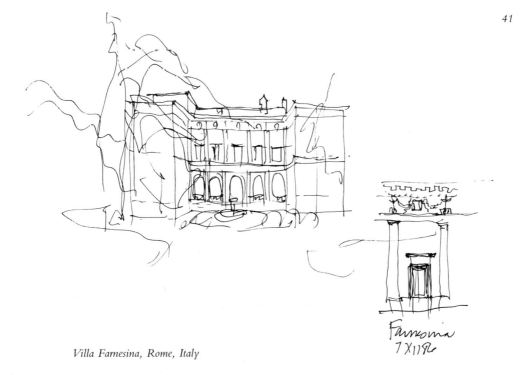

Villa Farnesina, Rome, Italy

DEAR DONLYN,   One more device that modulates (this time a vertical surface) occurs to me, although it has fallen into disuse in the past several decades: pilasters and the panels between them. They form a system for marking off a rhythm on a wall, relating it to the size of nearby objects, improving its apparent proportions, or for measuring a surface too long, enlivening a surface too blank, tracing a web of relationships that mean something to us across the face of buildings. One of the first chores of ornament is to create a visual structure, with rhythms and syncopations that satisfy the mandates of the composer, laid over the masses that use decrees. On the lovely delicate facade of San Miniato al Monte in Florence, for instance, the semblance of an arcade delineated in white and black marble sets a regular welcoming beat across the base of the church while a ritual temple form, framed again by pilasters, accents the high central mass of the nave. On the other hand, the patterns of Karl Friedrich Schinkel's Schauspielhaus in Berlin, for example, interweave a smaller and larger system of pilasters and entablatures to set up at once a fairly intimate scale and a grander one on the larger face of an urban building.

Michelangelo used a similar device earlier, when he was commissioned to replan the top of the Capitoline Hill in Rome, seat of the city's civic government. On the Palazzo Conservatori and its twin across the piazza, Michelangelo arranged a series of Corinthian pilasters over a smaller series of engaged Ionic columns. The composition is an impressive arrangement, where the colossal order dignifies the important building, while the smaller order relates the openings to a human scale. More-

43

San Miniato al Monte, Florence, Italy

Schauspielhaus, Berlin (after Karl Friedrich Schinkel)

over, the large pilasters seem to carry the weight of the entablature, and the rest—windows, bays, and columns—seems to hang from the travertine frame.

The pilaster is also used to transform the scale of a building's facade. What is large can be made to look smaller, or what is grand can be rendered more humble. For instance, at first glance Bernini's little church of S. Andrea on the Quirinale Hill does not seem necessarily large nor grand. It is a simple composition: two flat pilasters with Corinthian capitals frame a protruding round porch and support a classical pediment. Bernini's design is so effective that the pilasters diminish the apparent scale of the facade. The flat pieces of stone provide no details or clues of the building's dimensions; rather, one has to look at the doors to discover the pilasters' true scale. Then one realizes the colossal nature of the formerly tiny church, as the pilasters dwarf the celebrants.

Pilasters don't have to be flat, though, as Borromini proved in so many variations on his buildings. Pilasters with their strangely wonderful capitals are squashed into corners, or bent out around them. Sometimes they are plastered one on top of the other for a pilaster with many edges and folds. In other instances they are bent and curved so as to follow the twists and turns of the Baroque walls they adorn. And finally, they can be carved with wide flutes, in order to move the eye with ease from the floor to the fantasies nesting in the capitals, entabla tures, and domes up above.

Palazzo Conservatori, Rome, Italy

Wainwright Building, St. Louis, Missouri

But the Baroque is not the only place to find memorable pilasters. As mentioned, the neoclassicists used them in great variety and detail. In the age of the modern, the pilaster is transformed according to new manifesti and materials, and generations of pilaster cousins, nieces, and nephews are born. Although the evolution changes the appearance of familiar motifs seen in the classical past, the new pilasters still perform the same tasks. They still give an overall order to the facade, they provide a rhythm for the lines of windows, and they convey a feeling of support for the structure.

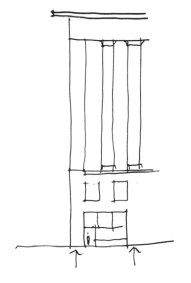

One good example that comes to mind is the Wainwright Building in St. Louis by Louis Sullivan, built just before the turn of the century. Here the pilasters (every other one of which is actually the cladding for a pier) rise for seven stories, as if a classical pilaster had been held at both ends and stretched until long and skinny. Both the tops and bottoms have intricate Sullivanesque terra-cotta decorations, and the pilasters' bodies are made of brick for texture and scale. In between, richly detailed spandrels bridge the gaps, creating a basket weave of sorts throughout the wide facade. From the street, when the light strikes the pilastered surface, the windows and spandrels sink into dark shadows, making a street wall of powerful texture and modulation.

Yet another modern and more recent expression of the pilaster can be found on many of Mies van der Rohe's buildings—the Seagram and Lake Shore Drive Apartments, to name a couple. These may be the most distilled versions of the pilaster, being slender I-beams welded and stacked on top of each other, stretching up into the city skies. What a far cry from the more familiar pilaster, but what similar functions. The thin strips rigidly articulate the glass surface, and they wrap the boxes in a uniform cadence of bronze or steel.

Chichén Itzá, Mexico

THEMES   *Platforms that Separate / Slopes that Join / Stairs that Climb and Pause*

• DEAR CHARLES, The ordered measurements of an orchard that we have described reach sideways, not just forward, to set things in position. In so doing, they establish relationships that are more abstract than an axis is, not dependent on the observer's eye contact with a distant object along a designated path. Changes of level introduce still another dimension of differentiation in position.

It is common to associate height with preferred status: "at the top of the hierarchy," "I'm the king of the castle," "top dog," "on high," "ascending." Or, one is "down," "downtrodden," "in the pits," "subjected." To some extent these hierarchical distinctions correspond directly to the conditions established by being above or below the surroundings. Being above one sees more, there is greater scope to one's view, it is possible to anticipate and one stands out, one is exposed. Being below often means carrying the burdens of what's above. It may also be more secure, more protected, on stable ground. These distinctions do not accost us with every step that we take, but they're present at some level in our response to changes of position up or down, even when the motivations for changes of level are quite pragmatic.

These distinctions can be used with great subtlety, as they are at the Taj Mahal where variations of level enliven the choreography of passage along the central axis, or in the thousand-pillared *mandapas* of south India where hierarchy is established within the orchards of columns by raised platforms, where the most sacred images are located.

The change of level may be small, as in a step or in the base to a throne, or it may be severe, as in the ramparts of a town. Platforms, areas that have been made level so that we can move across them effortlessly, are so ubiquitous in our urban civilization that we take them for granted, forgetting that they have been made. The floors we stand on separate us from nature, the terraces we look out from are raised up from the ground with great effort.

In Italian hill towns, built at the top of steep slopes, flatness becomes precious. Only by living in Urbino for awhile, traversing its slopes, did I come to fully appreciate how much we depend on and assume the ease of movement that flat surfaces provide. Until the late fifteenth century there were no outdoor public areas in Urbino that were flat: all streets sloped with the hills. The only flat surfaces were the floors inside buildings and a few terraces built up within the walls of family or convent compounds. Flat courts and terraces were the province of the privileged, and even these came in small portions. When Federico da Montefeltro enlarged his family's compound to make the great Palazzo Ducale of Urbino, this changed. Not only did he create a great hall of unprecedented size, the floor of which must have seemed an astonishingly large, smooth, and level uninterrupted surface, but he created a great level courtyard, nearly square, around which the rooms of the palace were organized. Another, more private walled courtyard was built out over the edge of the slopes as a roof terrace, situated above large vaulted chambers containing stables and a cistern below.

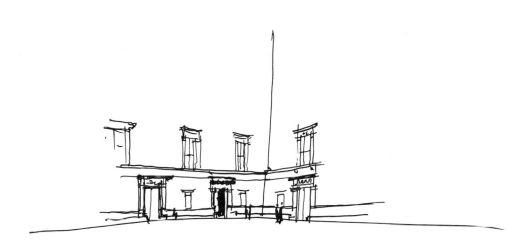

Palazzo Ducale, Urbino, Italy

Most innovative of all, however, was a flat terraced plaza that was created between the palace and the cathedral. Refined and delicate doorways (several of them false) fronting two sides of this level platform gave it the appearance of an open-air receiving room outside the walls of the palace, a large level gathering place that was open freely to the people of the town.

Montefeltro also had an enormous terrace built outside the city gates to create a flat marketplace at the lowest level of the town, where the road from Rome entered. The masonry walls supporting this terraced Piazza Mercatale are in some places as much as 40 feet high. An ingenious spiralling ramp was built inside a bastion at the corner of the Mercatale to connect the plaza and stables with the garden and cellars of the Palace directly above.

Not until the nineteenth century was another large flat area built in the public spaces of Urbino. At that time the

gardens of the ducal palace and the bishop's palace were cut
through by a flat road and an accompanying arcaded promenade
that connected a newly formed plaza, the Piazza Repubblica,
with an opera house and a park, formed in the old gardens.
This linear network of level places and passages then became a
locus for secular social and commercial activity, the strolling life
of the new urban middle class.

     In Siena, on the other hand, the great gathering place
of the community is a formalized slope. The Campo, perhaps
the most famous of hill-town piazzas, is formed in the
downslope of a valley cupped between curving ridges that connected three villages, each on its own hill. As the town formed
into a single entity the field between the ridges was captured as
a large half bowl facing the Palazzo Pubblico along its bottom
edge. In the fourteenth century this was shaped into a regular
surface and paved in brick. Its upper rim is ringed by bollards
that mark off an area that is mostly level. During most of the
year this area forms a promenade past tables that spill out from
the bordering restaurants. Twice a year, though, the tables are
cleared, and the outer ring is layered with sand so that it can become the course for the Palio, the spectacular semi-annual four-
minute horse race that stirs the disparate communal loyalties of
Siena neighborhoods and attracts visitors from around the
world. The bowl shape of the Campo makes it so that even
when jammed with people, as it is on such festive occasions, all
can see over the middle to the Palazzo Pubblico and to the assembled citizens all around. On more ordinary days the great
bowl of sienna-toned brick is used as a playground and place of

respite. In the summer Northern tourists even confuse it with a beach, setting themselves out to sunbathe in scanty suits on beach towels. The great slope of the Campo tips its users into view of each other and joins them together in a memorable communal scene.

Campo, Siena, Italy

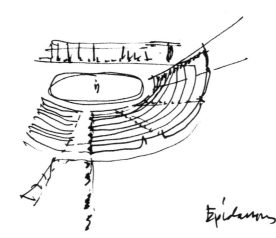

Amphitheater at Epidaurus, Greece

The Greek amphitheater is, I suppose, the most perfect fusion of levels and slopes. In a place like Epidaurus each step sets its row of citizens apart in an orderly way, creating clear views for all, without the jostling and confusion of a natural slope. The stage is a platform apart, a large level surface for action, that gives a freedom to those who have been designated to act or speak, which is denied to those delegated to the rows. The semicircular form focuses attention, and when sited in the hollow of a hill, gives a geometry of purpose to the underlying form of the land. These steps embody multiple significances as they serve witness to the play of ideas acted out across the stage.

(Incidentally, the stunning stepped clarity of the theater form and its capacity to bear witness must have been in Guilio Camillo's mind when he created the image of a Memory Theater with a sector of each level imagined as a drawer in which could be stored the ideas of one branch of learning.)

Michelangelo, who understood the use of nuance in form better than almost anyone (witness the pilasters you referred to earlier) used changes of level both boldly and subtly to shape the Piazza di Campidoglio in Rome. The summit of the Capitoline Hill had from ancient times been a place of great importance in the public life of the city. It regained special significance in the sixteenth century as the political power of the commune became differentiated from ecclesiastical power. Michelangelo's clever use of the odd angles already existing in the site to make a trapezoidal space facing the Senate building has often been remarked. So also has its relation to the earlier tapered plaza in Pienza. More to our point is the way in which he manipulates levels to give both coherence and vibrancy to the space. It is bound together by an oval inset in the trapezoid, with its outer rim set down, as though the surface of the oval were the top of an enormous egg. The summit of the hill is not flattened but made smooth beneath our feet. At the high point

61

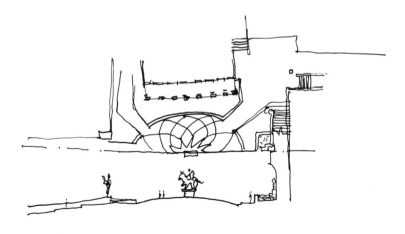

Campidoglio, Rome, Italy

Campidoglio, Rome, Italy

63

Campidoglio, Rome, Italy

in the center stands the beautiful equestrian statue of Marcus
Aurelius, suggestive of the administrative and artistic accomplish-
ments of Ancient Rome, and the wonders of a civilization that
belonged to that place. Around the edges of the oval there are
six differing segments that make up the rest of the piazza. On
the end facing the city is the entrance—a broad landing at the
head of a long, sloping stepped ramp that joins the Campidoglio
to the streets of Rome. To either side on the long sides of the
ellipse are paved terraces that are raised up a few steps. On
them sit two palaces with recessed loggias, each in turn up a
few steps from the terrace. Between these buildings and the Senate building at the opposite end of the ellipse are two passages
that slope down again to either side off the summit of the hill.
Directly ahead is the base for the preexisting Senate building, its
front transformed by a heroic set of steps that ascend to either
side along its face, ending in a commanding platform high in
the center of the building. Directly terminating the axis at the
plaza level is a fountain with ancient river gods sculpted on
either side. There a large molded wall makes a ledge to hoist
oneself up on. Nestled against the wall you face out across the
mounded oval, along the surfaces of Michelangelo's beautifully
modulated facades, past Marcus Aurelius, to the skyline of the
Eternal City beyond.

• DEAR DONLYN, We mustn't forget the quintessential
platform, the Athenian Acropolis, which is arguably the most
important place in the world. It's obvious, as Osbert Lancaster
noted long ago in *Classical Landscape with Figures,* that the
Acropolis is central in our memories of the ancient world, while

Acropolis, Athens, Greece

Mt. Lykabettos, standing next to it, and something like three times as high, is not mentioned once in the surviving literature, and is scarcely noticed even now, presumably because it comes rather awkwardly to a point, while the Acropolis provides—is— the platform on which Western civilization had room to be born. The subtleties of the place are well known, from the carefully choreographed climb up the hill to the Propylaea, where the effect of the buildings on each turn of the path seems to have been considered: windows and doors are centered between the columns from the point of view of the person approaching, not in the abstraction of the plan; below the smaller columns alongside the entrance porch, the bottom step is made of dark stone like the black-clad figures, symbolically invisible, who change the scenery in a Japanese play. The dark stone step allows the remaining ones to maintain the same proportional relationships with the columns above as the full flights (all steps white) maintain with the larger columns above them, flanking the gate to the top of the hill: the platform.

The gate to the platform is of course the climax, for me the consummate moment in all architecture. There you are, with the Parthenon as close as it can get and still be comprehensible as an object, with the complexities of the Erechtheion balancing it on the left. Much has been written of the subtleties of the arrangement by people trying to account for the magic of the place: of the wall that must, in ancient times, have withheld the full view of the Parthenon's facade until the visitor was close upon it, yet able still to take in the whole facade, glowing in its ancient colors. Constantin Doxiades has a fascinating theory, elaborated in *Space in Ancient Greece,* that the point in the

Propylaea where the view unfolds (and I, for one, get weak in the knees) is the center of a radial grid on which the corners of the visible buildings are located, so the view of the platform is ordered, closed, complete, and breathtaking. The space itself, the platform, rides above the city then and now—long ago a defensible bastion, and for millennia now a powerful monument, the center of the city and (for some the world) held aloft, special and separate.

The subtly modulated hilltop platform in Athens figures as center stage in the history of the beginnings of Western civilization—when I first saw it I could hear the voice of Pericles (miraculously speaking in English, of course) still ringing among the stones. The mountaintop platforms of Machu Picchu in the jungles of Peru are an altogether different matter. Dizzyingly and thrillingly dramatic, they pierce the mists above the Usumacinta River, the quintessentially hidden mountain fortress, providing their safety aloft, accessible on foot with difficulty and all but inaccessible to the intellect. The place is partway between the composed and altogether human constructions on the Athenian Acropolis and the soaring palaces of the imagination that spring from, say, the Grand Canyon of the Colorado. The difference probably is in the ornament—the message that the bold Doric and delicate Ionic orders on the Acropolis hold, refined and perfected over centuries to make manifest the values and enthusiasms of the culture they represent. At Machu Picchu there is a personal quality to the stonework, where decisions, inscrutable to us but carefully made, and heartfelt, caused the giant boulders to be cut and fitted (perfectly fitted), just the way they were. But we don't know enough to make sense of it, and

Machu Picchu, Peru

there is nothing figurative that speaks to us fellow humans across the gulf of time and place, hardly any more clues than the marvelous buttes jutting out of the Grand Canyon offer to us. All the same, the platforms in the sky, in their sheer dizzying verticality, their separation from the rest of the world beyond the mists that swirl below them, form objects to dream upon, phenomenological hiding, as from an eagle's eyrie.

Vézelay, an ancient Burgundian town, is at once platform and slope, a village tight against a simple street that climbs
from a square at the bottom up the long incline to a luminous
Romanesque pilgrimage church at the top. It is ringed around
behind by terraces sheltered by a grid of trees but open, over
the waist-high terrace wall, to a stirring panorama out and over,
the Burgundian landscape. The formula: an orchard of trees,
grass, benches, a sheltering building behind and a splendid broad
view out over the edge and down, is repeated over and over in
the hill towns of Italy, France, Spain, and elsewhere in the
world, and it always seems to work, to attract townspeople and
tourists alike to stroll along the edge of the platform.

Vézelay was an important pilgrimage center in those
years just before the end of the first millennium, when people,
anticipating the end of the world, sought salvation in pilgrimage

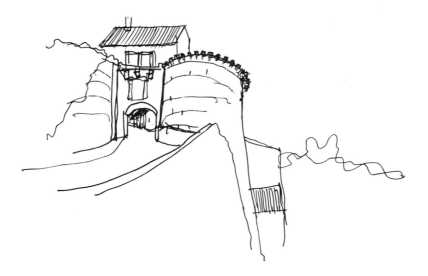

Vézelay, France

to holy places. They would first have seen the hilltop from the valley below, the lofty terrace backed by the church on its aerial podium, but then the church passed out of view, in the closeness of the streets of the sloping town, not to reappear until the little square at the top of the town was attained, where the west front of the church burst into view. The slope had rejoined the pilgrim with the eminence he had first looked on from far below. The exhilaration must have been immense: St. Bernard preached the Second Crusade from here, and it is tempting to suppose that the ascending of the slope that joined, to the platform that separated, enhanced the participants' crusading zeal.

The notion of platform is taken quite differently at Varanasi, on the banks of the holy river Ganges of India, where countless steps descend to the river in syncopated flights, with numerous platforms set amidst the stairs, each platform providing the private, separate setting for someone in an act of devotion. Here are all the lessons you could hope to have about interval and variation, about slope transformed into increments

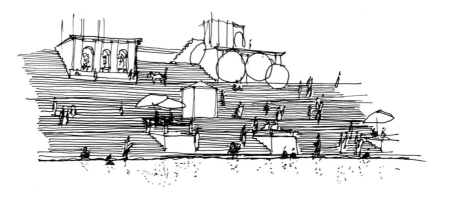

Varanasi, India

of level. One takes a boat to head down the river with a view of the platforms (called *ghats*), marvelling at the combination of cultural and spatial arrangement that cloaks multitudes of cele- brants exposed on the separate platforms in their individual wrappings of privacy. The frivolous but profound dictum about English cattle also strikes the mind: there is no such thing as a bad composition of cows on an English hillside. Just so, no combination of humans enshrined on their platforms in the nicely rhythmical variations of the riverfront steps is anything but moving and correct. In complexity, I think one could as- sert, is the chance for life; in extreme complexity the chances are extremely good.

• DEAR CHARLES, In the realm of complexity stairs have a special value, though they are a two-faced coin. On one

140 feet...

Steps, San Francisco, California

side they offer wonderful op- tions for playfulness and expres- sion; on the flip side they are among the most heavily regu- lated of building elements, precisely because they are so intimately tied to the body's physical movements and capabili- ties. The lift and depth of a step may vary only within the nar- row range of dimensions that will accommodate the size of our feet and a comfortable expenditure of muscular energy in hoisting the body one step at a time. Yet within this comparatively narrow range there is still a considerable latitude—in steepness, ranging from a gently stepped ramp to a vertical ladder; in width, ranging from the snug fit of a ship's cabin ladder to the expansive reaches of the stepped foreground of St. Peter's in Rome (or the cascading steps behind the apse of Santa Maria Maggiore); and in direction, ranging from simple straight-shot run to dizzying spirals. The choices made within these ranges, combined with the intervals of pause provided by landings along the way, determine the choreography of vertical movement through space. In emergencies, however, choreography is not a priority; predictability is. That's why the formulas for enclosed fire stairs are so prescriptive and mundane; for the most part they should be. Yet the lockstep that is appropriate in exit ways should not inadvertently become the standard for all movements through a place.

Stairs when set loose from the confines of emergency planning can move people through space in ways that touch the very fiber of our sense of self. We know through our bodies when movement is effortless and dignified, when it is choppy and confused, or when it acquires an unusual character signaling the approach to a place of special importance. The steeper a stair, the more likely it is to provide access to private places, to sleeping rooms and attics, for instance; or as in Mayan temples, to signify unapproachability. The wider a stair, the more generous and free the movement it accommodates, allowing for companionable ascent of several people at a time, or for the placement of people and objects along the way (liveried servants along the stair at Caserta, things requiring delivery from one

Steps, Piazza Grande, Arezzo, Italy

level to another at our house in Berkeley, toy soldiers being a bit of both in your house in Los Angeles). Stairs with frequent landings are especially gentle, offering moments of rest and visible connection points along the way. Stairs that twist and turn can provide shifting vantage points within the space they traverse (and, coincidentally, the opportunity for staged appearance), highlighting the opportunities for the choreography. Spiral stairs usually require so much attention to the placement of your feet that arriving at the top is a surprise.

It also matters what accompanies you in ascending and descending—an elegant thin steel rail with a wooden top shaped to your hand, crude openwork pipe rails with rough connections, or a stone balustrade with vigorously carved bulbous uprights and a broad continuous cap. Each sets the tone for your appearance in the building, the garden, or the street, and when combined with the choreography established by the stair itself, becomes visible evidence of the care extended toward those who experience the place.

The Spanish Steps in Rome can serve as an example of such care—larger than life normally allows—but suitably inspiring. At their simplest, in plan, they are an elaboration of an axis connecting S. Trinita dei Monte to the Piazza di'Spagna below. At their most reductive they have been described as a means for enabling police surveillance of an undeveloped hillside that in the seventeenth century had become a notorious hangout for illicit operations. In their majesty they now provide the setting for one of the most lively places of informal assembly in Rome, where throngs gather in stepped array to watch each other or simply be there.

The axis remains, striding up the middle, over the heads of onlookers sprawled across the steps. Most likely, the illicit activity is at best muted, but conducted under the watchful eyes of the police and the world's cameras. What brings people to this place is not just sun and slope but an extraordinarily deli-

75

Spanish Steps, Rome, Italy

cate fusion of the rhythms of human movement, the nuances of landscaped forms, and the chastening disciplines of classical orders. Symmetry about the axis provides the starting point for a very subtle reshaping of the slope's curving contours, but the axis itself is marked only by an obelisk at the top, the most forward points of two terrace walls, and the center line of very broad steps that stretch across the base of the slope. The stairs begin their descent from the church uneventfully enough, as paths cut between walls leading off in two directions flanking a balustraded outlook terrace opposite the church. They descend at a gentle slope into a large balustraded landing that curves across the site. The stairs turn out again toward the edges on either side, then curve down toward each other, merging into still another landing, this one leading into steps that spread all across the slope. As they merge, the steps on either side are faceted, one face leading subtly toward the center, the other turning slightly toward the edges to follow the spreading outer boundaries of the site. These various moves that formed the land are sculpted with great subtlety, highlighted by the steps themselves, which are undercut so that the layers are emphasized, and by curving stepped platforms that divide the lower stretches into wide center and edge paths and provide places for clusters of people to sit and for hawkers to spread their wares. At the bottom these platforms give rise to stone globes on pedestals, which, allied with a curving set of threshold steps, announce the beginning of a splendid ascent.

Vézelay, France

THEMES

Borders that Control / Walls that Layer / Pockets that Offer Choice and Change

Borders distinguish inside from outside. If they are simple, they make it clear where we are; if they are complex, encompassing distinct pockets of space, they afford choices or the chance to change. Since the ancient Egyptians built their temples, one of humankind's most potent devices for achieving mystery, distance, and the setting apart of a special place has been to build layers of walls—buildings within buildings, wall around wall like the successive skins of an onion. In architecture, as in thought, simple tight boundaries are most often too confining.

D E A R   D O N L Y N ,   People, like birds and wolves, have always been intensely territorial: birds, I read, sing to mark out their territory (everything in sound of that song is theirs); wolves use, less ingratiatingly, the odor of their urine to circum-scribe their place; and humans mark their territories with flags and towers at the center and at the edge with borders and walls. Borders sometimes control access and just about always make clear the edges of our domains (unless our domains get out of

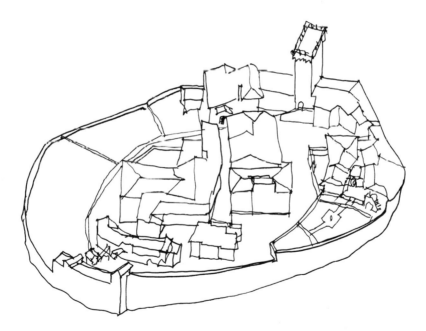

The Castello di Gargonza, Italy

control, like modern cities, and sprawl borderless into the vulnerable countryside).

Ramparts, of which the Castello di Gargonza in Tuscany has a peerless set, made appropriate defenses when the threats to security were more local than they are now, and still make a powerful enclosure for the imagination, the finite center that lies at the top of the heart of most fairy tales. A very few bigger cities have kept their bounding walls intact, and their visible limits move us still: Avila in Spain and Marrakesh in Morocco are famous examples.

Boundaries sometimes have been developed and dramatized from the inside. Some fine Georgian rooms come to mind; they establish the limits of the space as they insist on the shape of it and on the unbroken wholeness of it. Every wall has its integrity and is relieved, given motion and life by the openings in its doors and windows, but is never violated where it is vulnerable, as at its corners, or its cornice. Practice allowed a continuous floor plane to sweep beyond the boundaries of the room, which might even get a bordered rug or carpet to reinforce the regularity of the floor surface and keep it from bleeding out the openings. The ceiling might get a cornice to border it, and insist on its shape, or its regular shape could be further emphasized by traying the ceiling, or coving it, or repeating the bordering mouldings. The walls are composed, one by one, perhaps with borders for the rectangles of solid walls, or with pilasters to meter the spaces along the wall, and then divide into a rhythm of panels, in order for them to assert the presence, the regularity, even the sanctity of the boundary wall.

The enclosure is such a powerful action that inversions of the system, like mirroring the corners so as to seem to break the room apart, gently but surprisingly, can shock by denying a vision of the room as regular enclosure. Another wrench to the Western expectation of the carefully composed bordering room is the traditional Japanese effective removal of the wall plane to

Japanese house

wipe out the boundary in places, to blow through it to infinite or at least greatly extended space. The traditional Japanese blow-out of boundaries is especially dramatic as the absence of fixed furniture lets the tatami flooring suggest an infinite extension out across the landscape, the end of the indoors marked only by shoji, rice-paper panels that slide aside, and are even removable in good weather, so no frames even begin to establish a boundary plane. Some modern Western buildings, like the house your father designed for your family in Malibu, seek the same limit-less sense in parts of their borders, achieved in the twentieth century with large sheets of glass in thin metal frames, so as to allow thermal comfort all through the year without restricting the view.

A completely different attitude is developed in some Baroque work, especially Francesco Borromini's where the boundary is folded around the space and developed in folds and curves. Borromini's S. Ivo della Sapienza in Rome uses curves to make the folds of the six-pointed star into incidents on a con-tinuous undulating plane that makes of the church's boundary a faceted, ornamented, folded, varied, but in our minds continu-ous surface that celebrates the seamless circumvolution of the space.

Gardens too in most places are enclosed, sheltered from the winds across the desert or from neighbors and casual ma-rauders. The Garden of Eden had boundaries, and the very word "paradise" comes from the Persian word for walled gar-den. The format remains from ancient times: a source of water

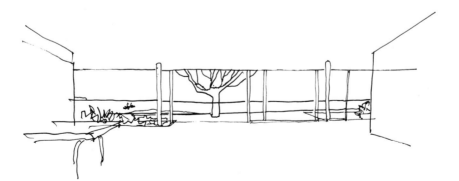

Maynard Lyndon House, Malibu, California

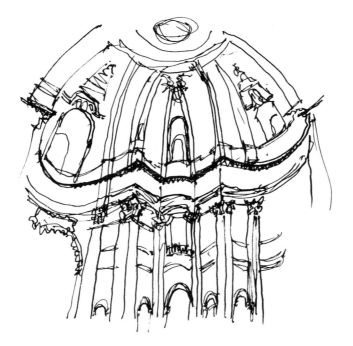

S. Ivo della Sapienza, Rome, Italy

in the middle, channels out from it in the four cardinal directions, flower beds in the quadrants, and, decisively, an enclosing
wall. Medieval gardens in the West, often tiny, had their bounding walls, and the idea of a "secret garden" hidden from view
until it is disclosed in a dream is central to our fantasies.

• DEAR CHARLES, Boundaries, their securities and
their transgressions, play a role in our dream lives, I suspect,
because they are so ubiquitous in our waking lives. Ubiquitous
and subtle; many of the borders that daily control our actions
are almost subliminal, absorbed into our routine responses.

Take, for instance, curbs. On a scale of grandeur they lie at the opposite end from city walls, yet the control that these six-inch borders exert over cars, pedestrians, and surface drainage is essential to the functioning of most segments of the modern city. Only marginally higher on the scale of grandeur are the bamboo hoops that Japanese gardeners use to keep the visitor from wandering off designated paths.

Next up in scale are the picket fences of the idealized American small town. Lined by fence or not, the edge of the sidewalk in these towns forms the border between public and private realms and limits areas of responsibility and access. Local custom concerning the transactions across that boundary do a great deal to determine the specific character of a place. Streets trimly bordered by neat white pickets, by patterned or wildly abundant flower beds, by approachable turf, or by solid garden walls, become, respectively, places that are dominated by a sense of public decorum and display, places for casual neighborhood play, or bounded places of passage with little invitation to neighboring.

Walls, however, make the most definitive borders, whether to a courtyard, a building, or a city. One of the images that has always been helpful to us in discussing our work is that of walls that make layers of space, with views through openings that overlap layer upon layer into the darkness or out to a view.

Surely walls that layer must be included in this Memory Chamber. The image that stays in my mind is not that of a building, but of the drawing you did once for a show at the University of Maryland concerning "Metaphors of Habitation." In that drawing you layered openings of various sizes and shapes

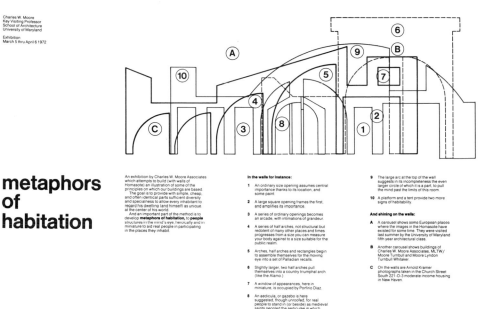

Charles W. Moore
Key Visiting Professor
School of Architecture
University of Maryland

Exhibition
March 5 thru April 6 1972

metaphors
of
habitation

An exhibition by Charles W. Moore Associates which attempts to build (with walls of Homasote) an illustration of some of the principles on which our buildings are based.

The goal is to provide with simple, cheap, and often identical parts sufficient diversity and specialness to allow every inhabitant to regard his dwelling (and himself) as unique at the center of his world.

And an important part of the method is to develop **metaphors of habitation**, to **people** structures in the mind's eye, heroically and in miniature to aid real people in participating in the places they inhabit.

In the walls for instance:

1   An ordinary size opening assumes central importance thanks to its location, and some paint.

2   A large square opening frames the first, and amplifies its importance.

3   A series of ordinary openings becomes an arcade, with intimations of grandeur.

4   A series of half arches, not structural but redolent of many other places and times progresses from a size you can measure your body against to a size suitable for the public realm.

5   Arches, half arches and rectangles begin to assemble themselves for the moving eye into a set of Palladian recalls.

6   Slightly larger, two half arches pull themselves into a country triumphal arch (like the Alamo.)

7   A window of appearances, here in miniature, is occupied by Porfirio Diaz.

8   An aedicula, or gazebo is here suggested, though unroofed, for real people to stand in (or beside) as medieval saints peopled the aediculae in which they stood.

9   The large arc at the top of the wall suggests in its incompleteness the even larger circle of which it is a part, to pull the mind past the limits of this room.

10 A platform and a tent provide two more signs of habitability.

And shining on the walls:

A   A carousel shows some European places where the images in the Homasote have existed for some time. They were visited last summer by the University of Maryland fifth year architectural class.

B   Another carousel shows buildings of Charles W. Moore Associates, MLTW/ Moore Turnbull and Moore Lyndon Turnbull Whitaker.

C   On the walls are Arnold Kramer photographs taken in the Church Street South 221-D-3 moderate income housing in New Haven.

89

Metaphors of Habitation (poster drawing)

in elevation as though they were on successive surfaces. The juxtaposition of shapes and the suggestion that bands of space might lie between them made this single drawing suggest an architecture that would reward exploration.

What made this image so suggestive, when there are few places that are actually made with openings syncopated that way? I think the answer is fairly simple—the drawing brings out in a static image what happens to us all the time as we use and experience places. Whenever we look out a framed window we see parts of a larger visual field, traces of another order, arbitrarily cut off by the confines of the opening. Then, as we shift position just a little, the field of vision changes; what we can see is altered and the juxtaposition of shapes is different. When there is a porch or a set of trees or a succession of rooms through which we can look, the dynamic shifting of views that takes place as we move can become quite pronounced—even, sometimes, thrilling.

What's more, what we can see through such layers is distinctly affected by how we move and look, by our participation in the place. It places initiative in the hands (or feet) of the observer.

This is a large part of our fascination with orchards, I think, and certainly accounts for my inordinate fondness for diagonal views across cathedrals and churches, where rows of columns lining the nave and side aisles appear to intersect in syncopated intervals as you move along the aisle, then at the transept crossing lead off in several directions at once.

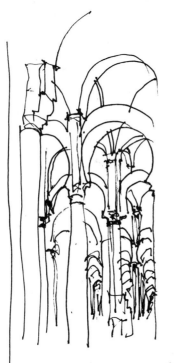

Great Mosque at Córdoba, Spain

But buildings of smaller scope can also be suggestive in this way—provided they have some thickness. The dynamic shiftings and layerings of views and outlook that occur when we move through space simply do not normally show up in elevations, drawings constructed as abstractions. Such drawings purposefully discount the vagaries of perspective vision, dependent as it is on an observer's specific position in space.

Alas, all too many architects have presumed that the abstractions of the elevation are the real thing, and have produced buildings whose walls have no thickness—no overlappings are possible, and there is simply one plane of transition between inside and outside. By eliminating the nuances that make it fun to move from one place to another within a set of spaces, such buildings severely diminish the pleasure of choosing your own positions within the structure.

There's another type of layered wall that must be noted, even though it may seem entirely different. In these it is time that is layered, not space. Streets in European cities, especially in Italy, are often bounded by such walls, masonry structures that show the traces of successive stages of construction, decay, reconstruction, and alteration.

In the walls of Rome fragments of ancient stone carving suddenly appear in the midst of freshly cast plaster, tapping out a rhythm wholly independent of the building's present uses. In Italian cities built first in the Medieval period, then rebuilt during the Renaissance, large areas of wall are like superimposed game plans: sweeping relieving arches of masonry are interrupted disrespectfully by elegantly framed Renaissance

Colosseum, Rome, Italy

openings and latter-day windows of convenience. Following the trace of disparate building campaigns through these walls can lead the mind back through layers of time to expand the evocative power of the place. Layers of this sort cannot, of course, be fabricated in an instant. Yet we know a lot about the buildings that have preceded us and the people and conditions that made them, so dimensions of time can also be included by reference.

For our present purposes it seems important to construct an illustration that will make us all remember to make walls that leave room for improvisation and choice; walls whose openings allow people to choose various alignments—to pick their position among layers of building and landscape, graduating from inside to outside and beyond. Places of this sort are likely to have niches and nooks that can be claimed either by inhabitants or by their cherished objects, so that the whole becomes filled with people and their semblances; rather as the townscapes depicted in Tuscan paintings are teeming with incident (and symbolism) or the walls of a Moghul palace are layered with niches and inlaid representations of the vessels, vases, and flowers that might have been found there when court was in residence.

Walls of this sort that offer a diversity of opportunity and suggestion give room for reflection and appropriation. They allow us to think about the boundaries of space in several ways and to make them our own, either by filling their niches with objects of personal use and affection or by using their symbolic suggestions, and the outlooks they afford, to build up a personal understanding of the place.

The boundaries of our common public space, as we have noted before, proffer similar opportunities for reflection and appropriation, though generally in a looser way. The gardens, lawns, and porches that border the streets of a traditional American town are filled with the evidence of individual families making choices; each family in its own way creating places for play, languor, ritual, maintenance, and display. Where these borders have been made indifferently, as a mere requirement of zoning with the repetitive decorative trivia that mass marketing imposes on whole tracts, they offer little to our lives, whether

6th Street, Berkeley, California

we are residents or visitors. When, however, the spaces between buildings and the street are made more definite and varied, with fences, walls, hedges, and terraces and with insets and projections and purposeful displacement of buildings, the resulting distinct pockets of space tend to become filled with imaginative attention. The residents of houses along the street adapt their spaces to their own particular uses and aspirations, and visitors to the place find their passage bordered by the intricacies of individual human care, offering both visual stimulus and social—one is tempted to say anthropological—insight.

The same may be said of urban street walls, public places whose boundaries are made by continuous rows of buildings brought to the edge of the public right of way. Where those borders are perceptibly thick, allowing for many types of interaction, they can be immensely satisfying: thus the universal appeal of sidewalk cafes and outdoor displays, the pleasures of show windows that change with the seasons and give free previews of the offerings inside, or the relief provided when a recessed entry gives sheltered respite from the flurry of movement and transaction—or rain.

NAYBAION
C.V.MOORE

Village street, Greece

Borders can be thrillingly abrupt when they strike the edges of grand differences; the city and the sea, the protected and the wild, the sacred and the profane. But when they reflect territorial claims that are ultimately negotiable, when they take their place in the midst of human transactions, they should generally be layered and interwoven, thick with opportunities for reconsideration.

Port Angeles, Washington

Portals bid us welcome and draw us through them. Doorways and gates cultivate expectations of the places that lie beyond. Windows in a wall, like the eyes of a person, allow us to imagine the life within. From inside, windows and other openings can frame a view, editing out unwanted parts, emphasizing the wanted ones. A well-framed view brings the world close; clumsy muntins thoughtlessly push it away.

• DEAR CHARLES, If borders, mostly walls, set the territory for a place, it is the character of their openings that most directly affects the experiences they afford. Openings and their location determine the pattern of connection between one room and another, between inside and out, between light and dark. Seen from outside, it is the openings in a wall that strike the strongest rhythms across its face, and that narrate the life within, either directly, through the activities they reveal (as in a

2   View of courtyard looking toward common room.

University Avenue Housing, Berkeley, California

glazed storefront), or by inference, through the pattern or shape of windows that suggest the nature of spaces behind: tight and small where privacy is paramount, more expansive where common uses are involved, broad expanses of clerestory for artists, blank for telephone substations.

The placement of openings therefore is a matter of great importance. They must be considered in at least four ways: as ways to move and/or see from one space to another; as sources of light, air, and sound; as voids in the structured fabric of a building; as a pattern that explains the character of a building and suggests comparison with buildings of similar ilk. All too often buildings meet the demands of one of these considerations too simply and at the expense of the others.

In most traditional Western buildings the solids of the building, the masonry or assembled wood products joined together, serve as a tight boundary clearly differentiating inside from outside. They keep out the undesirable rain, wind, and marauders, creating chambers of quiet and predictability within. Openings within or between solids translate the tight boundary into a system of flexible control.

Generally, the solids also serve to transfer weights to the ground, collecting the forces generated by the roof, beams, walls, and floors above and channeling them into the earth. The voids in the building fabric must, of course, be organized so that they do not disrupt this flow of forces. For masonry construction this can be a demanding discipline, one the master masons of the Gothic period transformed into an astonishingly delicate art. They reversed the order of dominance from solid

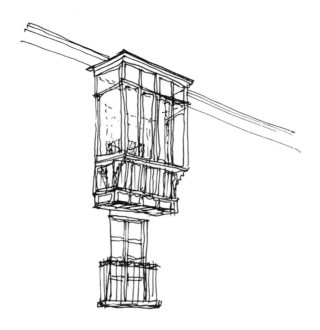

Windows, Toledo, Spain

to void to create interiors with unprecedented qualities of light and freedom of movement. Where earlier masonry construction had generally used walls as membranes that absorbed forces and distributed them willy-nilly to the ground, the Gothic master masons, like contemporary wooden barn builders, applied a pattern of linear analysis to the building mass and created a framed system of openings. The Gothics pushed this analysis to the extreme to give themselves greater opportunities to create transparent walls and spacious halls. The history of architecture could be written in terms of an ideological and technical struggle between the membrane and the frame, with differing cultures weighing in differently on the balance between solidly opaque and flexibly open, based partly on materials available, but more fundamentally on how definitively inside was to be separated from outside.

Presently most large construction makes use of a frame to limit construction costs, then secures the separation of inside from outside through an independent membrane. This separation of structure and skin was highly celebrated in the middle of this century, leading to the ubiquitous glass-walled facade that often pointlessly equated structural opening with transparency— whether or not there was reason to see from one side of the membrane to the other (and often when there was plenty of reason to demur). These doctrinaire glass skins of the twentieth century often missed another important aspect of an appropriate system of openings—the ability to control and modulate the passage of light and air.

Story has it that Louis Kahn, when Resident in Architecture at the American Academy in Rome, spent what seemed to his colleagues an inordinate amount of time in his room admiring the nuances of light. Adjusting the numerous filters available in a Roman window would have made this possible. These include a pair of casement windows that can swing in, ranging from cracked ajar to altogether open, and an independent pair of shutters on the outside that can similarly swing more or less out. These have small slats that can be adjusted from horizontal to vertical, allowing subtle modulation ranging from filtered light entering directly in, to light bouncing up toward the ceiling, to no light at all. Finally, there's a much simpler set of controls inside, with solid swinging flaps that can be used to cover the surface of the glass to a greater or lesser degree. The variation and subtleties that attend the use of these several filters are wondrous indeed. Open and closed are simply not the only choices that should be available to us in the boundaries with which we surround ourselves.

Window, Palazzo Farnese, Rome, Italy

Openings (windows especially), the sizes and shapes they take and the intervals between them, are among the most useful tools for composing the face of a building. One very good measure of window size, attributed to Alberti, is that a window should be large enough so that two people can have a conversation beside it. The shapes of windows identify, generally, the nature of the spaces behind the wall, their relative size, their need for light or privacy, and their position in a hierarchy of rooms—identical, as in the ubiquitous strips of a faceless

S. Maria in Campo Marzio, Rome, Italy

109

Facultée de Droit
7 VI 87

Faculté de Droit, Paris, France

office building; subservient, as in the narrow windows of a bath-
room; grander than the rest, as in the special bays for a front
parlor or the rose windows in the nave and aisles of a cathedral.

Playing with variations in openings to establish a basic
underlying rhythm, adjust sizes, and create incidents of special
interest—tracing on the building's surface a story of the life
within—can be a great pleasure, bringing the architect close to
the spirit of a composer or a writer of narrative.

The greatest pleasures, however, are those that come
when the openings of a place structure the experiences within,
as at your house in Pine Mountain. Working at the dining table
there, I was struck by the ability to have at the periphery of
my view (and therefore readily available for distraction) three
different views into the pines; one on my left through sunlit tall
trees to the blue silhouette of hills beyond; one down through
the living room below and out the windows precipitously to
the adjoining canyon; one to my right across the table to a
sunny deck and a thicket of backlit pine needles. The left and
right openings are each, somewhat predictably, sliding doors
opening to broad decks, paired, though on opposite sides of the
dining area. They make the space wonderfully light and flexible,
allowing access directly to a choice of sun or shade at virtually
any time of the day. They also provide a continuous balance of
light in the room and capture breezes from either side. The
view down, on the other hand, is an extraordinary one and
could have been lost in so many easy ways: the dining room
might have been sealed off from the living room, hence no
view; or the openings between the rooms might have started at
a conventional handrail height of 36 inches off the floor, hence

House, Pine Mountain, California

no view down; or the large windows set low on the right side
of the living room wall might instead have been placed in the
middle of the wall, slavishly conforming to convention and sim-
plifying the structural calculations, hence no view down the
canyon. Yet it is that precipitous canyon view, more than any
other, that is indelible in my memories of the place. Without
those large low windows in the corner, the whole alliance of
openings and stairs into a continuous passage along the east side
of the house descending to that view would have been diminished, if not pointless.

Openings that frame views are not always windows;
they may be dramatic gaps in the building fabric itself or openings within a series of garden walls. In Toledo, Spain, the major
plaza is elevated, close to the edge of the town. At midpoint
along one side the arcaded buildings that shape this urbane

space give way to a grand arch that frames a view of the stark landscape beyond, thrusting a reminder of the harsh realities of the land into the civilities of cafe and bodega chatter.

At the Santa Barbara County Court House in California an even grander arch is opened in the side of the building near the entry to offer passage into a spacious inner lawn court

County Court House, Santa Barbara, California

Sketch of Portal Site, Washington, D.C.

and to frame a compelling view of the mountains beyond. This single great gesture brings together into one view the coastal mountain setting, the echoes of a Spanish heritage, and the Anglo civility of a comforting lawn. With a few steps forward you add to the view a highly picturesque jail and a terraced stage for community festivals fronting the lawn. Openings of various sorts modulate the surrounding building walls, some of them small and concealing, many giving on to open-air passages that connect the courtrooms, all of them artfully considered as aspects of the county seat. Borrowing inspiration from Santa Barbara we imagined, for the so-called Portal Site in Washington, D.C., a framed portal to the Capitol that would have served to organize development of the site, structuring experiences of the place around the central image of the city.

• D E A R D O N L Y N , With the arch at Santa Barbara and your Washington proposal, you bring us into the realm of portals, which not only open the view to this world and beyond, but actually welcome the entry of the participant.

This act of welcoming, and of giving some message about what to expect—uplifting or downright scary—has been, for most of the civilized past, one of the important functions of architecture. It waned a little during the twentieth century, when a common complaint about modern buildings was cast in terms of one's inability to find the front door. Before that the art of entering a place received considerable attention: Egyptian sculptors carved portals in the sides of stone tombs, accessible only to the spirits of the departed. The doors, which soon received supplicants, announce aspects of the world within, or beyond. Ghiberti's doors to the Baptistry in Florence are

West Front, Chartres Cathedral, France

Roman Forum, Rome, Italy

perhaps the most famous, but some earlier masterpieces (my own favorite are the doors of San Zeno in Verona) more simply display the wonders of the shared memories of the initiated.

The message needn't be right on the portal; at Autun, for instance, the spot above the doorway is where the message is captured with a magnificent Jesus organizing the divisions between heaven and the far more kinetic action of hell. On the front of Chartres, more powerfully still, the columns flanking the portals serve as supports for a gathering of straight and very architectural saints of stone.

The portal has the strength, even, to come off the buildings and stand alone. Roman triumphal arches were made initially as a place for conquering heroes to march through and the rest of us, usually, to skirt or simply observe. In Japan, the torii accomplish this, as they stand on their own to symbolize the importance of entry. Rather simpler and more standardized than a Roman triumphal arch, they can rise on occasion to great poetic heights, as in the giant torii that stands in the water on the tidal flats of Itsukushima, on the Inland Sea of Japan, where the location restricts passage, mostly, to the navigator.

Far more modestly, the front doors of residences (in some cities especially) bespeak the qualities of the house inside. There is a popular poster on the market made up entirely of enticing Georgian doors in Dublin. The little city of Stonington, Connecticut, accumulated, in the early nineteenth century, a distinguished collection of front portals of modest size and not much depth, secure in the general agreement about what a portal should be like; but each one is unique, the product of a craftsman's care applied to that special place.

Some other times the portal calls for a porch, to make the process of entering be something that occurs in time, however short. The American front porch used to be, before the days of air conditioning, a special place where the family could sit in private in the public realm, to take the air and connect in a gentle way with the neighbors. In some cases the porch became a site for display of ingenious and energetic geometries as well as for the figures of resident family members.

The wood that was used predominantly in American domestic architecture from the mid-nineteenth to the early twentieth century lent itself especially well to fanciful display

Bungalow porch, Texas

and to the creation of transitional structures, neither inside the house nor entirely outside. By turning wood members on a lathe to get variations in profile, drilling flat boards with patterns, or elaborating their edges with scroll cuts and then

Oak Bluffs, Massachusetts

Zimmerman house, Virginia

assembling bits of wooden structure so that they surround an axial path of entry (often extending it around the sides), builders
such as those who made modest little bungalows for the Meth-
odist Camp Grounds in Oak Bluffs, Massachusetts, invested
their decorative skills in porches that speak with a fervor and
imagination well beyond the means of the simple constructions
they introduce. As an ensemble of porches ranged along the
camp streets, they tell a lively story of spirited communal assent.

      Bill Turnbull's great latticed wall surrounding the Zim-
merman house in Fairfax County, Virginia, with a layer of sun-
sheltered multilevel porches is another case where the portal
transformed into an adventurous porch becomes the voice of
the house, its grand shapes echoing in our recollections of the
place. More conventionally, the porches of Seaside, Florida, set

Porch Buses, Alice Wingwall sketch

much of the cadence of the place, providing the usual blandish-
ments of fresh air in a tropical clime, overlaid here, as well, by
the pleasures of discovering how forthrightly correct and appeal-
ing the elements of earlier Southern architecture could be. Perhaps the most playful of porches would be those that Alice
Wingwall imagined for the Stratford Fragments, a collaborative
exhibition piece that we prepared for the Architectural League
in New York. Porch buses were devised (movable structures
akin to Volkswagen buses done up as stairs), along with portals
on wheels, that could be repositioned according to the course
of the sun, the temper of the seasons, or the current status of
neighborliness.

Porches can also be stern, formal, even intimidating in-
troductions to the institutions that lie beyond, as in the ubiquitous Classical pediments that front public buildings, proclaiming

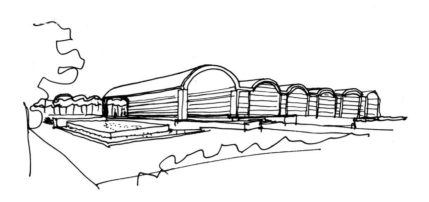

Kimbell Art Museum, Fort Worth, Texas

their legitimacy. Or, they can explain quite clearly the nature of the building inside, as they do at the Kimbell Museum, where the elegant structural modules of the building are laid bare in the open arrival porches—telling immediately and memorably of the scale, orientation, and structural clarity with which the place has been composed.

If the openings are the eyes of the building, then the portal is the mouth, the aperture most able to tell us about what is beyond.

121

Academy of Fine Arts, Philadelphia, Pennsylvania

Newport, Rhode Island

6

Roofs that Encompass / Canopies that Center

 *Flat roofs collect the rain, and too often let it in. Pitched roofs shed it and let it join the rest of the water flowing away. More than that: pitched roofs give the viewer some welcome sense of how big the building is that they sur-mount, and which way it extends. And they give the architect something dignified to compose. The roof is summarized by the canopy. For all of human history, aediculas—delicate pavilions with four columns and a canopy above—have been symbolic houses for Christian saints, Hindu gods, Jewish newlyweds, Egyptian pharaohs whose virility was being extended, and more recently for bands and bandstands and householders in their gar-den gazebos. We believe that an aedicular four-poster is one of the best forms to create the center of the world, even for a family on their own premises.*

T H E M E S   *Roofs that Encompass / Canopies that Center*

D E A R   D O N L Y N ,   The most exciting part of the building, for me, is the roof. In the first place, it describes the extent
and shape of the building, and even helps define its place in its
town. Then, too, it serves as a guide and a discipline for establishing the geometry of the plan, and helps bring some order to
the whole process of designing.

"Roofs that Encompass," literally taken, has to do with
the physical act of encompassing, covering the building, describing it; symbolically taken, it can tell us a great deal about the

Sketch for competition

use and worth of the building. The conventions were established long ago; the head man in an ancient Greek town was
entitled to a gable roof—everyone else's house had a flat
roof—and traditionally he sat between the columns of his front
porch and under the gable, to dispense justice and to rule,
strengthened by his position in the place made special by the
shape of the roof above. Centuries later, in Hellenistic times, as
aspects of divinity became mixed with the kingship, the live

Trinity Church, New York, New York

body was replaced by a statue, higher up just under the peak of the roof, in a "window of appearances."

The special silhouettes of domes and steeples and gambrels and hips and sheds, as well, help establish buildings as discrete objects with their own importances, and a specific extent: we can see how far the building reaches, and to some degree, what it is. One of the most highly visible and memorable aspects of any building is its silhouette, and a distinguishable silhouette confers some special importance on a structure. Trinity Church on Wall Street in New York, for instance, with its steep gable roof and spire has more presence than the skyscrapers that flank the canyon, and even the gabled temple of the Treasury Building nearby outclasses its much taller neighbors.

From the recognition that roofs describe the extent of the buildings they encompass follows the possibility of manipulating that description: roofs acting like brackets of emphasis can be arranged to make many buildings read as one, or a building

Jewish Community Center proposal for Trenton, New Jersey (after Louis Kahn)

larger than is thought desirable can be covered with a number of roofs. Louis Kahn's scheme for the Jewish Community Center in Trenton, New Jersey, was never built, but it has thousands of offspring; it described each major bay of a sizable building with a separate pyramidal hat. Kahn's Kimbell Museum in Fort Worth, Texas, similarly underplays any hierarchy of roofs with a series of identical parallel barrel vaults that separately admit light. The magic in that building (and there certainly is magic in that building), in which the slit vaults admit and reflect the light of the Texas day, alive with the passing shadows of fast-moving little clouds, comes partly from the demise of the encompassing roof.

Although I think the Kimbell is one of the greatest buildings in the hemisphere, my own particular fascination is with the opposite: the simple sheltering roof shape that encompasses multiple situations underneath. It started with our cabin for the Jobsons in Monterey County, California, in 1962, where a pyramidal roof falling all around from a skylit aedicula in the center of the tiny house allowed a mezzanine for sleeping next

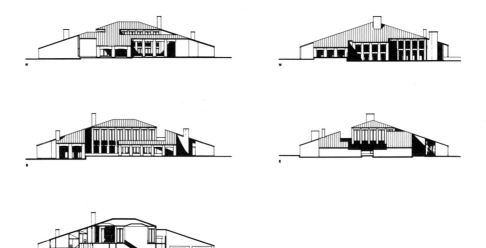

California Governor's Mansion Competition scheme

Johnson House, Racine, Wisconsin

to the four-post center, then dropped variously to a small dining
area, tall, with vertical windows facing into spiky redwood
trees, then to a wider, lower seating area with horizontal windows over a bench, then finally, lower still to a door facing a
deck that bridged a creek. We tried the same notion again, in a
competition entry (which did not win) for the California governor's mansion. Here a huge hipped roof was cut way back to allow windows in a high central reception room on the upper
floor, then extended all the way to low eaves over one-story
rooms and garages way out on the perimeter. In both schemes,
the roof describes the building and exercises a powerful discipline that directly relates location (distance from the center) to
height. We proposed an even larger hipped roof for a hotel on
St. Simon's Island, Georgia, called Xanadune (which was not
built), then finally, in 1989, finished a larger house near Racine,
Wisconsin, under a high hip that spreads out along the four di-
agonals from an upper living room to the four wings of the
house, lower as they spread.

Chateau rooftop, Chambord, France

Something should be said, too, for the wonderful materials that roofs can be made of, which locate them in our memories. The Mediterranean barrel tile comes to mind, and Nordic slate, sometimes huge, as in the Swiss Alps or in Norway; thatched roofs in Japan and the British Isles make sinuous, soft silhouettes. Then there are slick American shingles, which tend to be cut in fascinating patterns. Stanford White's Casino in

Neuschwanstein, Germany

133

Newport, Rhode Island, had at least five patterns of shingle on
its tower. There were long shingles on California barns, and I'm
partial to corrugated metal. One of my childhood fantasies was
to be given the commission to design the Episcopal Cathedral
in Port Darwin, Australia (where I still have never been) altogether out of corrugated galvanized iron sheets.

Then there are the fantastic roofscapes that have been
built; dream worlds of chimneys and turrets, like Chambord
(which we should include too, in Allies that Inhabit), where the
chimneys stand tall and seem almost human as they populate the
rooftop space, or like Neuschwanstein, romance-besotted Ludwig II's fairytale palace, that reminds us how universal is our imagery, as well as how richly varied: everybody knows what a
fairytale palace looks like, as almost every child across the world
can draw a house, snug under its roof.

• DEAR CHARLES, In discussing this Memory Chamber,
we must remember what it is like to be inside—under the roof.
What we see overhead can be a powerful means for establishing
position. The center of a dome, the crossing of vaults, the intricacies of a structural frame that visibly carries weight to one side
or another, are all means through which we can judge our location in a structure.

Historically, the patterns established overhead have
been especially potent in this regard because the upper profiles
of a space are usually clear, visually unencumbered by the people, furniture, and equipment that normally obscure the boundaries of the floor. The edges of a vault or a dome or three-

dimensional shape overhead are easy to grasp and conceptualize. You will remember that in the *Place of Houses* we noted this, and observed also that intricate or symbolic shapes embedded in the space overhead did not interfere with the everyday actions of people on the floor below. "Keep the myth up off the floor," we suggested, and let spaces develop extra interest and meaning without clogging the arteries of function.

The shapes of a space above, especially when they are high above, are clearly visible, but they are outside the normal cone of our perspective vision. As a result they require attention, often the physical act of tipping the head. They lie outside the ken of normal operational vision, but they are uncommonly vivid and dynamic as we look up to shift the center of attention and locate ourselves within the volumes that the shapes imply.

In buildings that are built to stack people and uses many layers high on a small site this potential is diminished, and architects often forget to consider the ceiling as anything more than the bottom of the floor above or, more accurately, the bottom of a plenum given over to the engineers to fill with unsightly structural members, ducts, pipes, lighting, and sprinklers. Yet even in high-rise office spaces the overhead surface can be an effective place-making device, once it is rescued from the spatial oblivion so prized by engineers. Coffers and shallow vaults can be carved into it in strategic locations, creating vestibules or emphasizing special landmark spaces that help to make a perceptible substructure of positions within the general flow of work spaces.

Volumes of space that reach from the earth to the underside of the sky, like primitive huts and celebratory domes,

Pazzi Chapel, Florence, Italy

have a special power to mark our position in the world. With its dome, pendentives, vaults, and circular medallions, for instance, the Pazzi Chapel in Florence nearly hums with the music of the spheres. Vaulted spaces are no longer frequent in our world, yet their expressive potential is used still to give special meaning to important places, or it is simulated in large entry halls that give borrowed identity to towering stacks of less fortunate rooms.

One of the greatest twentieth-century spaces of this sort is the great vault over the concourse of Grand Central Station, replete with a ceiling studded by down lights laid out in constellation patterns. The space is so lofty, the scope so grand, that it has become one of the principal public spaces in the city, a nodal point in anyone's map of Manhattan.

Great rooms of this scope are not frequent in the city, nor should they be. There can only be a limited number of focal points even in a great city. The Winter Garden at Battery Park City in Lower Manhattan is a more recent attempt, where a very tall glassy atrium slides out from the bottom of two towers. The glass gallery that spans across its breadth filters sun and light into a fairly amorphous space, one that leaks off into several levels of shopping and out through glass walls onto the promenade. Glass atria of this sort make for very dramatic spaces, for the sort of shock value that burns a sensation into the mind; but the transparent image is vague, unmeasurable. This is probably deliberate, given the general merchandising impulse to make retailing spaces indistinct and to borrow the influence of any landmark spaces for all the adjoining establishments. The purpose of these spaces is to envelope the complex in a shimmering image of light and spaciousness, not to create a clear generic center of the sort that has been dominant in the traditions of architecture.

The greatest of the great canopied rooms, in my book, is Hagia Sophia. It's not coincidental, of course, that it was built in the service of what seemed then the greatest of ideas. Built by Justinian in A.D. 532–537 to honor the Christian God, it served later as a sacred space during the several centuries that it was an Islamic mosque of the Ottoman Empire.

The transcendence of Hagia Sophia's spaces has little to do, however, with the doctrines espoused within it. It results, rather, from the astonishing audacity with which its builders arced masonry across space, creating a sequence of interlocking vaulted volumes that encloses a vast volume. The surfaces, clad in glass mosaic, are almost like continuous softly gleaming membranes, severed at the base of the uppermost dome by rays of light that stream through a ring of openings. This uppermost canopy, so far above the floor, is the constant point of reference for experiences of the place, the obvious culmination of all the vaulting effort, the surface that the eye constantly seeks as you

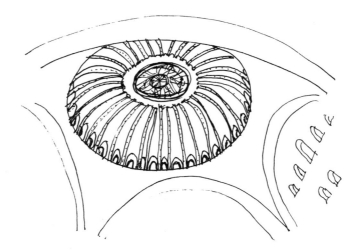

Hagia Sophia, Istanbul, Turkey

Hagia Sophia, Istanbul, Turkey

move through the space. It is the geometry that holds in the mind even as you pass under subsidiary vaults and around massive piers.

Nothing is more centered than a dome; all its surface refers to the focal center point. When it is very high, shallow, and large, as at Hagia Sophia, it becomes an enveloping presence, lending a protective aura to everything underneath. When it is lower and smaller—a diminutive canopy—its center is more precisely focused, a locus that can be occupied by a single person. E. Baldwin Smith observed that early representations of

Moghul Tomb, India

canopies in Ancient art were depicted as ceremonial covers carried above the heads of chiefs and kings, offering both shade
and status. The geometry of this relationship of canopy to center to occupant is so fundamental that it recurs in many cultures, as for instance in the many-domed tombs of Moghul

Hindu shrine canopy

architecture, where externally the domes become markers that magnify the presence of the royal body in their midst, or the miniature aedicular shrines of religious architecture, where four posts and a canopy (or their representative equivalent in carving or paint) frame the image of a saint, spirit, or sacred location.

Miniature canopies lead us back to the aedicula, and to Sir John Summerson's discussion of the subjunctive in architecture—the "as if." In his essay "Heavenly Mansions," he sketched the history of the use of miniature representations of architecture within architecture. The wall paintings of Pompeii, he observed, were replete with fantasy structures, mostly skeletal follies of columns, lintels, arches, and canopies. These devices carried over into niches to house mythical figures, thence into ornamental schemes for illuminated manuscripts and on through them, he contended, into Romanesque architecture—setting in motion the system of niches, tracery, and vaulting that led eventually (and with a lot of help from many other forces and impulses) to the elaborately skeletal Gothic, where each bay of the many-layered structure can be imagined as a surrounding of four posts with a hovering canopy above; the whole becoming a heavenly city—airy, multiple, and radiant.

Summerson likened the recurrence of such motives to a childhood attachment to play, to fashioning fantasy houses out of grown-up furniture (pianos were his example, though tables and chairs with sheets draped across them may be more common in current practice). Children claim, thus, a world their own size, magnifying their presence in the larger world where generally they don't quite fit.

Shore Temple, Mahabalipuram, India

In architecture similar devices were used to bring to mind large and expansive realms, like heaven, that were otherwise hardly manageable. Nor was the practice limited to the Classical tradition and Christianity. The forms of a Hindu temple tower are elaborated with intricately replicating miniatures arranged so that they provoke at once the semblance of a holy

143

Shore Temple, Mahabalipuram, India

city and associations with the sacred mountains that culminate in Mt. Meru, apex of Hindu mythology.

The power of a structure brought close around, as in the child's playhouse, is, however, more than associative. Bringing the elements of a structure palpably close increases the sense of a building's embrace. The effects of perspective also cause the elements close at hand to play a dominant role in your field of vision—dominant, but unstable; by looking away or changing position you can obliterate or alter the impact. Being within a diminutive structure, then, magnifies the importance of your movements. It's another way of being king of the castle.

Akbar's tomb at Sikhandara, outside Agra, capitalizes on both these aspects of the aedicula. A great work by any meas-

Akbar's tomb, Sikhandara, Agra, India

ure, the structure is an extraordinary merging of Indian traditions; the Hindu ones indigenous to the place and the Islamic ones more recently imported by Akbar's forebears. The tomb is a stepped pyramid, the edge of each level marked out by aedicular pavilions, spaced to give prominence to the corners and the center of each side. In this it conforms to the fundamental or-

ganizing pattern of Hindu temples, laid out on a cosmic man-
dala diagram and developed in receding stages, with varying
forms of manipulation at the cross and diagonal axes—sometimes they are built literally in the image of a stepped pyramid
with little huts all around the edges. Here in the tomb for this
most synthesizing of Moghul rulers, the huts are replaced by
elegant four-post pavilions more readily identified with Islamic
palaces. They are airy structures, handsomely endowed with
a canopy and carved detail and more suggestive of cooling
breezes, poetry, and dalliance than of dark and mysterious primal forces. They make, indeed, splendid places from which to
look out over the garden; delicate, personable structures open
to the surroundings, each defining a separate center, yet arranged in obvious compliance with a larger order, one with
which the well schooled could encompass the cosmos.

The top level of the tomb is different than all the rest,
walled at its outer edges by an arcade and delicate white marble
perforated grills. It is inward-looking, empty (but for two sar-
cophagi), and sequestered, whereas the lower levels are red sandstone and outward-looking, with a massive impenetrable center.
The icy, singular perfection of the upper-level court, screened
from the world outside, contrasts knowingly with the multiple
miniatures and playful silhouettes of the lower platforms, and
still more with the great cross-axial and once abundant garden
in which this miniature cosmos sits.

Summerson also suggested, in "Heavenly Mansions,"
that the aedicula was a thing of the past; that modern architecture was too squarely in tune with the real problems of modern

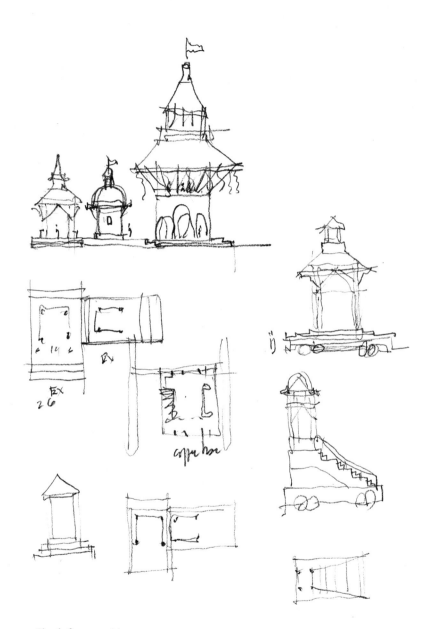

Sketch for competition

life to waste any energy on imaginative play. We thought not
then, when the wonders of the aedicula sent us scurrying off to
embed them in our various works. And we think not now—
thirty years later, when the power of imaginative play seems
even more central to serious work.

Olympia, Greece

7 Markers that Command / Allies that Inhabit

 Monuments, towers, obelisks, pyramids, and the like command attention and mark a center. They lay claim to space and give us something to be next to. There is a danger of being inflationary, when too many competing markers trivialize and obscure the ones that really matter. On a more intimate scale, objects the size of people—furniture, statues, columns, even chimneys—become fellow occupants. They help us inhabit places and stand in for us when we're not there.

● D E A R C H A R L E S , Borders that circumscribe an area
may be the most secure and definitive means for controlling a
territory, but markers are the most obvious. Flagpoles, obelisks,
and towers all stand up to be counted, as also do roofs if they
have enough shape to matter. As surrogate inhabitants they lay
claim to the land by commanding attention, marking the center
of a realm.

Gargonza, as you point out, has a peerless set of ramparts, precisely and severely limiting its perimeter. They establish it as an entity, and strictly control the experience of the
place, from both inside and out. Yet it is the severe, storybook
silhouette of Gargonza's tower that stakes a claim on the
surroundings.

Not that its tower is so very special or unusual in its
shape; it's a perfectly ordinary nineteenth-century reconstruction

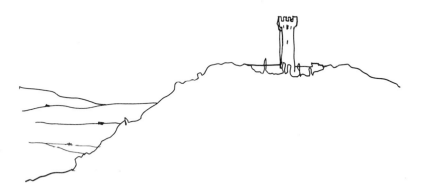

Castello di Gargonza, Italy

of what a Tuscan tower should look like. The point is it towers; it stands up over the town where it can be seen from (and watch over) afar. Its defensive utility, like that of the ramparts, was once crucial, but now it serves mainly as an identifying mark, the locus for measuring one's position in the place, or for gauging time by the thrust of its shadow.

A much more elaborate, taller, and more elegant tower sets a comparable mark in the symbolic heart of Siena. Here, though, the tower rises from a hollow rather than from the crest of the city's hills. The Torre del Mangia, by climbing out of the Campo to such an extraordinary height, manages to become equivalent in distant silhouette to the startling hilltop figure of the cathedral dome—a matter of some consequence, we may presume, to the proud oligarchic government that built it next to the Palazzo Pubblico. We know that Siena's powerful families were acutely aware of the commanding presence of towers, so much so that many families built them to express their standing in the community. We know, too, that when the commune meant to punish a family severely—for treason perhaps, or maybe for an inappropriate political alliance—it pulled down their tower. Vengeance being addictive, very few towers remain and none to disrupt the tense equilibrium between the Torre del Mangia and the cathedral.

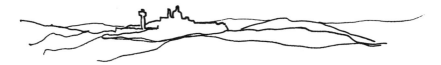

Skyline, Siena, Italy

San Gimigniano, Italy

   In nearby San Gimigniano, however, clusters of towers remain to give that city its unforgettable skyline; a jumbled juxtaposition of thin masonry shafts that rise high above the city's roofs. In their disordered majesty they are akin to the temple complexes of Khajuraho and Bhuvaneshwar in northern India, where temple towers cluster together in pantheistic assembly The masonry towers of San Gimigniano are room size and hollow. Those of northern India are nearly solid, containing no rooms for human use. They are markers pure and simple, the embodiment in stone of the life powers of the little stone god figures housed in square cells beneath them. Singly each lays claim to its immediate domain, in multiples they create an assembly of presences, a field of intense energies and mysterious significance.

   The *sikhara* towers of Hindu temples evolved into shapes that were particularly effective as markers, commanding attention through their distinctive silhouettes and extending the

Sikhara, Bhuvaneshwar, India

force of the command through the miniaturized repetitions of
the form that are used to modulate the corners and surfaces of
the structure, bringing reminders of the dominant silhouette
down close to worshipers at the base.

   The Hindu city of temple towers bears some resem-
blance to the skylines of our present cities, with office towers
jostling each other for position. In the Hindu complex the hierarchy is clear, though, and in our competitive commercial skylines it certainly is not.

   The contemporary commercial tower is most often vic-
tim of a mixed message. It is tall, therefore inherently a com-

manding presence, an object wishing to be proud. Yet in most American downtowns it is one among many, the type with which the city is built—ideally a building wishing as well to be a neighborly citizen. To be a marker, a building must be set off from others, with a free-standing silhouette from afar, and usually an intervening space when you're near. As a result a spate of commercial office towers were built after World War II with vacant plazas at their bases, separating each off from the other and creating a street of disorderly, conflicting, and hollow commands. In the 1920s many architects got it right, constructing buildings that were at once distinctive in the skyline, with a slender marker tower reaching up to identify their location, but the bulk of the building built to the street edge, helping to

United Shoe Machinery Building, Boston, Massachusetts

shape the common spaces of the city, hardly distinguishable from neighboring walls. There's great civility in this approach; a distinguishing marker to announce a building's presence in the city, but not to command the attentions of everyone passing by on the street. The United Shoe Machinery Building in Boston is one of my favorite examples, and the Chrysler Building in

Chrysler Building, New York, New York

Coit Tower, San Francisco, California

New York City is still probably the most elegant, a building whose tapering top is so vigorously and gracefully shaped that it has become a landmark for understanding the city, but whose walls at the bottom partake gracefully in the cadence of Manhattan's streets.

Buildings that should really be set aside as markers are ones like Coit Tower and the Ferry Building in San Francisco. Coit Tower, atop Telegraph Hill, marks a most splendid public outlook spot, arguably the emotional center of the Bay region. The Ferry Building played, and plays still, an extraordinary role in the city, as embarkation point for the commuting ferries that

tied San Francisco to its surrounding Bay Area communities
before the bridges were built. Thousands of people entered
through its passages and linked up outside with the streets and
streetcars that led people up through the city. It's a vigorous
tower, uncommonly tall for the time and set right at the end of
Market Street, an appropriate marker for this crucial place in the
city. Its placement, on axis with Market Street and apart from
other tall buildings on the waterfront (city regulations have limited heights on the water's edge) make it stand, still, as a distinctive civic marker even though San Francisco now has a
superabundance of big, tall volumes.

• DEAR DONLYN, These markers pure and simple introduce the most dramatic and characteristic silhouettes of our own
century—skylines—made of towers that have another function:
to multiply by scores the available floor space (for hotel rooms
or offices) on a given site. But the bonus from a distance is the
memorable shape of the big city. New York is the most famous:
observe how the graceful towers carry the image to identify the
city. Note that it is the top of the towers that make the silhouette and identify the place and its qualities. At their bases the
towers work best to merge in the streetscape, as you've noted.
The skyline is an amalgam (an unplanned concatenation) of skyscrapers designed as individual markers. Some few are actual
markers, but most, especially the tallest, are "functional" spaces,
almost accidentally markers. The basis is part financial bottom
line, part chutzpah, part art—and connoisseurs seldom agree.
I thought New York was better before the World Trade Center

altered the scale with its high blunt towers to make the older arrangement seem diminished, even puny. But in Los Angeles the new First Interstate Bank, far higher than anything else, gives point and coherence to a skyline composition that had previously seemed quite pointless. San Franciscans are so self-conscious about the pieces that seem at odds with the rest (like the dark blunt boxes of the 1960s and 1970s—or for me the Transamerica Tower) that they have instituted an elaborate new method to exercise design control over the skyline; except for fostering towers like Siah Armajani's top for a not-yet-built Cesar Pelli building, the positive effects of this concern are not yet very apparent.

Seattle has a great skyline too, with a couple of especially high towers with eccentric shapes that cause them to compose with the lower ones around. And I'm especially fond of Houston's very tall buildings, satisfyingly compacted into a symbol of downtown for a city that doesn't have one.

There are only memories now of rides across the Southwest when most every town had a handsome new skyscraper (usually just one, so really a marker), thin and maybe twenty stories tall. Some, like the Luhrs Tower in Phoenix, are still visible, shouted down by recent thicker and higher blocks, but delicately graceful still.

It helps if there is a place to view the skyline from a distance—the bay in New York and San Francisco, the lake shore in Chicago, the waterfront in Hong Kong or Singapore. These multiple markers, these skylines surely form some of the most memorable images of our time.

Still in the realm of Markers that Command, I'm full of images of Seaside, Florida, which I've just visited. It is, it seems to me, a remarkably successful attempt to make a town by the beach with lots of images of familiar towns, like many of us grew up in. It is open to the charge, of course, that it wallows

Seaside, Florida

in nostalgia, and that its diminutive scale hovers on the edge of cute. But it seems to me for many reasons that it succeeds. And one of the most notable reasons is the skillful use of Markers that Command.

The houses that make up this carefully controlled and diminutively sized town lie just inland from the sea, and many of them raise cupolas—markers in the sky to allow the inhabitants to walk up onto a breezy deck from which they might view the town and the water. The ensemble is, I imagine, open to the criticism that the markers have multiplied almost out of control. Perhaps half the houses have an outlook or a tower or some form of marker in the sky. But somehow the impulse to mark the place house by house is so genuine and enthusiastic that it is easy to forgive the excesses and even to exult in them. As in the Castello di Gargonza, the impulse to climb up and see matches the impulse to be seen from nearby and from a distance. The belvederes are far more modest, say, than the towers in San Gimigniano, but fully as ardent and are one of the most endearing features of this carefully put together seaside vacation village, which aspires to be a town.

Sketch, pavilions

● DEAR CHARLES, Markers stake out priorities in a larger geography, standing in like flags for the territorial claims of an institution, an owner, or an idea. There are a number of elements that work similarly at a smaller scale, acting as surrogate inhabitants to fill a place with friendly presence.

Statues are the most obvious surrogate inhabitants for buildings. Most often when they appear in medieval or classical buildings they stand above, bearing iconographic significance, urging us to consider or remember some lesson deemed appro-

Palazzo Vecchio, Florence, Italy

Statue, Art Museum, Rouen, France

priate for the place. In doing so, they also set a measure to the place, indicating the size of persons, although their size is often inflated or diminished—as the power of the iconography or the purses of the patrons required. The confluence of sculpture and architecture has a long and varied history, one that was severed by the decrees of modernism and is now staging a still uncertain recovery. Florence is home to the most famous sculptural inhabitants of a city, symbolized by Michelangelo's David standing oversized and in perfect poise in the Piazza Signoria at the threshold of the Palazzo Vecchio, the seat of oligarchic power and civic pride. He and his cohorts add a dimension of time and heroism to the plaza; they make us, for the moment,

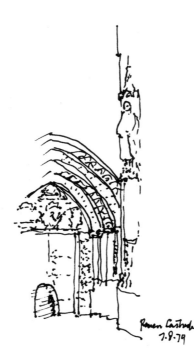

Portal, Rouen Cathedral, France

cohabitants of a realm peopled not only by our touristic counter-
parts in jeans and lederhosen but by figures of heroic proportions: the denizens of Hebraic mythology; the sculptors of
Greece who first gave perfect form to sculptures of the body;
Michelangelo himself and his contemporaries the Medicis who
spurred him on; and the citizens of the young republic, whom
the sculpture of David was meant to symbolize.

The likeness of William Penn, founder of Philadelphia,
plays a very different role in his fair city, situated not in the
street among citizens but perched at the pinnacle of the City

Hall tower, commanding the center of the city. Until recently city law decreed that no buildings could rise above him, setting in this particular place perfectly suitable limits to developer ambitions. No more; the limits have been broken and the city is now free to become an unfettered jumble of complex towers—like any other—though at least for the moment economic recession has diminished the ardor for building high.

Boston has an especially fine tradition of civic sculpture, properly sited to become allies in our appreciation of the city. Sam Adams, rabble-rouser and patriot, stands on a pedestal in the space between Faneuil Hall, home of much revolutionary rhetoric, and City Hall, the oversized newcomer to the scene. The Boston Common has numbers of notable figures standing about. The Boston Public Gardens have an exemplary row of civic worthies spaced between trees at the southern edge, while the promenade that strides across Back Bay on Commonwealth Avenue is interrupted at almost every block by some suitably instructive figure inhabiting the path. My favorite is the abolitionist William Lloyd Garrison, who sits in the middle of the path in a magnificent bronze chair on a podium bearing the inscription: "I am in earnest—I will not equivocate, I will not excuse, I will not retreat a single inch, and I will be heard."

More recent times have been less conducive to noble sentiment and suitable allies. Mags Harries wittily memorialized the everyday confusions of Boston's traditional open-air market at Haymarket by embedding cast bronze paper and vegetable litter into the paving of a street crossing there. Claes Oldenberg's abstracted Mickey Mouse enlivens the otherwise flat and barren plaza of Houston's Public Library with forms big enough to imagine playing inside of and a witty moveable tail piece that is connected to Mickey's body by a chain. Sculpture, whether wry or robustly rhetorical, implants the evidence of thought in our surroundings and allies with our wish to believe that places are built with human purpose and sympathy.

Villa Poiana, Italy (William Turnbull sketch)

Even more opportunities for such alliance are found in the shapes and sizes of openings and the cavities in a building's surface. These range from the niches in many nineteenth-century public buildings that still await their sculpted inhabitants, to the windows and doors of any building. They help us to imagine the people who use the structures of a place and animate their surfaces with signs of life. That elements of buildings that approximate the size of persons can be evocative is marvel-

University of Virginia, Charlottesville, Virginia

ously suggested in Bill Turnbull's Christmas card sketch of the
entrance to Palladio's Villa Poiana. Classical columns (not
skinny posts) are especially effective in this way; "personable columns," Alice Wingwall calls them. My favorite examples are
those that border The Lawn at the University of Virginia,
where Thomas Jefferson set a row of small white columns of a
Tuscan order marching along the edge of the green in front of
the student rooms. They are interrupted periodically by columns of a larger, grander order that form the porches of faculty
residences, which housed the professors of differing fields and

the classrooms they used. This assembly of columns establishes a domain of unparalleled civility and decorum—a blend of intimacy and measured aspiration that prevails even over the frisbee and beer parties that currently grace the "Academical Village."

More personable still are the bollards that ring the Campo in Siena. They are handsomely carved simple stone uprights perfectly scaled for leaning against or parking things by during most of the year, though sturdy enough to support the plank barriers that transform the outer ring of the Campo into a horse racing course at the time of the Palio.

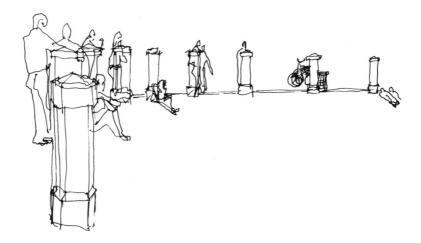

Campo 8.26.87

Campo, Siena, Italy

The processional quality of a row of uprights is, of course, nowhere more profoundly apparent than at the Parthenon on the Athenian Acropolis, where the close ranks of precisely fashioned white marble shafts encircle the sacred abode. Accompanied by a marble frieze depicting a ceremonial procession, they have created a place so resonant with care and purpose that it has captivated the Western mind. Jefferson recreated such a procession in a gentler, more varied way at the University of Virginia. Later, in the Jefferson memorial, John Russell Pope used, in turn, a stiffer, grander, and more archeologically correct version to surround a rotunda sheltering Jefferson's statue. At the even more austere Lincoln Memorial processional columns stand in for the ranks of tribute bearers and provide an atmosphere of dignity and solemnity that outlives the daily onslaught of T-shirts and snapshots—yielding a place that can serve still as a locus for the nation's most urgent public assemblies.

In Egyptian, Hindu, and Greek architecture the uprights, thick columns of stone and masonry, have frequently been intertwined with connotations of human (or more accurately divine) presence, resulting, for instance, in the seated Rameses that support the temple front at Abu Simbel, the columns in south Indian temples that are carved as though they split to reveal a god figure inside, and the mysteriously serene caryatids in the Erechtheion on the Acropolis in Athens, female figures who bear the architrave and roof of a curious porch offset to the rear and side of the temple, as though attesting to hidden uncodified powers.

The hearth and its attendant chimney are allies of a different sort—signaling not the body but the domesticated fire

Hearth, New Mexico

that is essential to feeding and shelter. The hearth serves as a point of gathering for family and friends, a symbol at once of human bonding and of connections to the primal energies of the world. The fireplace, formalized descendent of the open hearth, still bears enough of its magic (except when enclosed in energy-conserving glass doors) to help us inhabit a room. It serves routinely as the focal point for the chairs, sofa, and table, which recall human presence even when they are empty. In the grand manors of the seventeenth and eighteenth centuries, the

Stratford Hall, Virginia

fireplace surround and its mantel received the special attention
of craftsmen who framed the openings with delicate carvings
and the insignia of hospitality and refinement.

  Chimneys, each of which marks the presence of a
hearth below, can be vigorous allies in staking a place on the
land. As elements that must rise above the roof, they necessarily
figure in the building's silhouette. Located purposefully, they
can help to shape a memorable image, at once vigorous against
the sky and indicative of the spatial order within. Located aim-
lessly—as happenstance protrusions through the roof—they clut-
ter the image of the place. Your favorite example, the paired
clusters of chimneys at Stratford Hall in Virginia, are by far the
most compelling; they set their mark upon the surrounding
plantation in a singularly powerful way, each cluster forming
the four uprights of an aedicula, the pair of them marking two
wings of the mansion and bracketing its breadth at the peak of
the roof. The sculpted chimney that you and William Turnbull
used to focus the Rush House at The Sea Ranch is a more

Rush House, The Sea Ranch, California

Heil House, The Sea Ranch, California

modest but comparably powerful example, using the chimney silhouette to draw the building's form up into a powerful claim on the edge of the meadow. Turnbull's purported "lattice chimney" on the Heil House farther down in the meadow links the need for chimney height with the notion of a wind- and sun-sheltered widow's walk to transform a simple little gable house into a semblance of Stratford itself, an enthusiastic place marker on the slope toward the sea.

Marysville, Kentucky

THEMES   *Light that Plays / Shadow that Haunts / Shade that Lulls*

 *Space and form are understood in light. Light can clarify them, as the ancient Greeks knew, or it can extend and enhance mysterious distances, as did light coming through stained glass in Medieval cathedrals. It can move and change continuously the spots on which it lavishes its attention, as in southern German Rococo churches. Light can sparkle or dapple or slide across a surface or even flash from a neon tube. "The sun never knew how wonderful it was," Louis Kahn said, "until it shone on the wall of a building." We can't sense space without light, and we can't understand light without shadow and shade, which are different from each other. Shadow is the ghost of an object; shade, the absence of light, offers us refuge from the overzealous sun.*

• DEAR DONLYN, There is light, in which we discern all architecture, and then there are kinds and kinds of light that bathe architecture or just caress it lightly, or make it dance and play. Light defines space, and the accounts of space are phrased in terms of light.

It might be useful to describe three kinds of light, all the same phenomenon from the same source, our sun, and from some tiny artificial extenders of the sun's rays, filtered through three of the filters that define themselves in human memory. Let's call them Pagan Light, Mystic Light, and Light that Plays.

Greek temples, and classical moldings ever since, are bathed in the light of the sun, a source that rides across the heavens every day (some say in a chariot of fire), always changing but, in sunny climes, accurately predictable. Ancient peoples, especially the Greeks, fascinated by the nuances of their clear light, and by the newly discovered enlightenments of geometry, perfected a series of moldings that cast the shadows that gave order and life to the parts of their sacred buildings—base, columns, entablature, and tympanum. They even invented, initially, three versions of those, three "orders"—Doric, Ionic, and Corinthian—to differentiate moods and memories of some buildings from others. The robust muscular shapes of the Doric order depend on spare shadows that underline the convex swells of the echinus and the very columns of the order, full in their entasis, unaccented by any extra shadows at the base. By contrast, the gentle, less muscular, and more flowing shapes of the

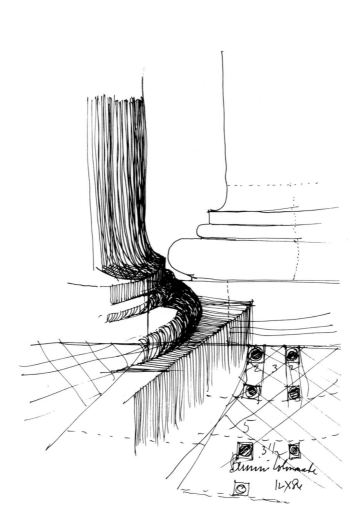

Colonnade, Piazza San Pietro, Rome, Italy

Ionic and Corinthian order are more elaborate in their chiaro-
scuro, in the sun-and-shadow complexity of their light. But
however veiled in mystery their ancient messages, their glory as
they stand in the Mediterranean sun is clarity, the brilliant precision of full light edged in shadow.

A very different quality of light appears in the mists of
the northern forests, which we'll call Mystic Light. We know,
of course, that the sun can shine brightly and clearly in the
North, and that Greek temples can be shrouded in mist, but
that doesn't seriously undercut the usefulness of characterizing
the prevalent moods of different lights. Mystic Light envelops its
object, so shadows are not sharp, and light glows (however
softly) more than it shines.

The stained glass, especially of the thirteenth century,
made use of the soft light of the North, and redefined for us its
magic. The architects dared to pile their small stones dazzlingly
high, in piers perpendicular to the plane of the wall, so the
walls were freed to be mostly of glass and very high. Then the
glassmakers devised pieces of unprecedented rich color, blues
and reds, and fashioned them into illustrations of familiar tales
and the shared memories of the initiated. The soft light of the
North comes through the incredibly rich reds and blues, and
they glow—ornament and message and a bath of light all at
once. The Sainte Chapelle in Paris, where stained glass predomi-
nates, is perhaps the most intense experience of mystic light,
though Chartres Cathedral has room for subtleties in the bath of
light. Henry Adams in *Mont St. Michel and Chartres* compares,
for instance, the north and south transept rose windows: in the
north, the gray light and the straight lines of tracery of King

Philip Augustus provide the basis for a robust geometry of sharp corners in the circle of the windows, while the King's mother, Blanche of Castille—who inspired the rose in the south transept—is honored with a more fluid tracery of curves, between which the sunlight sometimes shimmers.

Mystic Light still is caused to shine sometimes, but we are more likely in our time to encounter Light that Plays, though the most exciting examples were brought to life in the eighteenth century in southern Germany, most remarkably by craftsmen in stucco, the brothers Zimmermann at Die Wies.

That remarkable little church can usefully be considered as a box that seduces and bounces and teases and explodes the light. The light enters the white interior through big windows on the south, bounced perhaps from fresh snow on the meadow outside, and then reflected off thick white window frames to beam on to the paired columns that ring the nave. Each of these columns is flared out in section so that the light grows dimmer as it wraps around the column, then gleams forth for one last bright line before the column's surface falls back into the darkest shadow of all. The light doesn't glow or shine; it plays and surprises as it moves across the window frames, the columns, and the north wall of the nave. The tall figures of saints rise into the sun, and cast their shadows on the walls behind them. And again the light and shadows play, moving in remarkably quick time as a darkening shadow falls on St. Augustine, then slides across him until a bright beam strikes somewhere on the actively modeled surface, so that in a very short time the sun's rays light up something important, maybe a part of the face, and then play across, perhaps, a fold of drapery.

Ronchamp Chapel, France

In the nave the sunlight is dancing across white walls and
figures, with glints of gold. Ahead in the sanctuary are columns
and wall fragments, each one casting shadows toward the north,
but here the shadows fall on rich dark tones, deeper as the light
penetrates the sanctuary, to be absorbed as it wanders among
the hanging arched openings.

      The architects revered earlier in this century (like
Le Corbusier) saw their buildings in Classic Light, constant and
revealing. There is a special interest now in Light that Plays and
dances and changes, yet all the kinds of light are part of our
heritage, and all of them are available to us.

• DEAR CHARLES, Light, in all its subtle modulations, is exhilarating; the stuff of life itself made vivid to us by the surfaces it falls upon. Shade and shadow help us to measure the intensity and direction of light, emphasizing through darkness the radiance of the reflected sun.

Shadows are ghosts, the figures created by the absence of light. As in your description of Wies, shadows move, climb walls, inhabit corners, and are elusive. Shadows haunt the day and mark its passing. Shadows on buildings are like punctuation; small projections gain emphasis, rhythms are underscored, hollows and cavities are revealed, and all march to the same inexorable disciplines of time and geometry as the earth twists in front of the sun.

The most exciting shadows are those cast by narrow elements falling in recognizable figures across the surfaces of a wall or the paving of a street. Columns in a colonnade stand forth against the darkness behind them, their angular traces setting measure to the pavement between, sometimes striating the wall itself. In a place like Siena, the summer sun directly overhead throws a shape of building eaves down on the center of the street, weaving a jagged, narrow path of sunlight across the dark paving.

Torre del Mangia shadow, Siena, Italy

Later the same lines are drawn on neighboring buildings, creating a visible reciprocity that underlines the mystery of the city. The most compelling shadow in Siena, however, is that of the extravagant Torre del Mangia, which rises far above its surroundings and sends its shadow across the great Campo like the gnomon of a sundial tracing hours across the curved and sloped bowl of the piazza. The tower shadow is thick enough so that groups gather for a while in its passing shade, then either move with it or pass on. Its presence haunts the expansive brick surface of the Campo like a reminder of the narrow, shadow-inhabited streets that make up the rest of the city.

Sometimes, most obviously in places where the sunlight is fierce and unrelenting, shadow and shade are the desired qualities, the positive goal to be sought in making buildings or planting trees. The orchards we have discussed, with their stone corollaries in the Mosque of Córdoba and the thousand-pillared *mandapas* of India, have just such an intention in mind—to create great areas of shade removed from the direct heat of the sun. In the *mandapas,* which often have no walls, you know how deep you are in the building by how dark it is. The intensity of the shade around you is measured against bright sunlight at the fringe.

Shade is gentler than shadow: without figure. It is the absence of direct sunlight rather than the trace of its obstruction. A thicket of trees creates shade; arbors and pergolas that create a network of dappled shadows are built equivalents, especially suited to areas where trees cannot take root or where strict control is in order. Shade is mixed with reflected light and may take, therefore, some colors from its surroundings or be

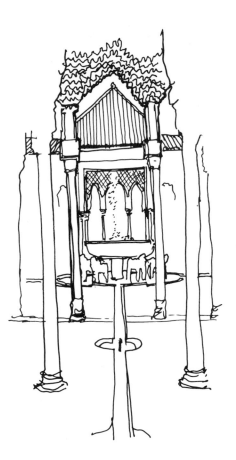

Alhambra, Granada, Spain

animated by the flicker of reflections from an adjacent pool, as
in the Court of Lions in the Alhambra. Earlier cultures were
very subtle about shade, treating darkness as a quality to be manipulated and articulated as richly as light. The most compelling
examples are inside Hindu temples, so dark in contrast to the
burning sun outside that your eyes take minutes to adjust. As
they do, a carved and articulated world emerges, all surfaces

modulated with imagery and moldings to retain an echo of the vitality that floods the temple's exterior. Even the ceiling is carved in intricate floral patterns recessed in layers to extract depth and vibrancy from the pale light reflected off the floor. Islamic architecture is also filled with surfaces that play on reflected light: tiles that glitter, moldings that rib surfaces with shadow and, most notably, intimate stalactite vaulting like that of the Alhambra that fills the absence of sun with the presence of ingenious craft and subtle modulation, elements of fascination to enliven the shade that would otherwise lull the mind.

● C O M P O S I T I O N S

S. Martin de Canigou, France

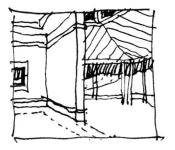 *Architectural space is different from the void of the philosophers. It is palpable stuff that can be chopped into neat and finite pieces, like Georgian rooms, satis-fyingly modulated, comfortably proportioned, and fully visible. But you can enjoy it as well—perhaps even more—if it escapes around corners or lifts up into light, releasing us from the claustro-phobia of the dark confines around us. The Baroque perspective of the Bibienas or of Piranesi pulls us into themselves, then up and out, while they dazzle our imaginations. Space is the archi-tects' medium and its manipulation our most rewarding task.*

COMPOSITIONS | *Rooms that Define / Space that Leaks Up Into the Light*

DEAR CHARLES, The themes we've so far described are all crucial to making places and giving them a character that is memorable—a character that connects mind to matter. The most fundamental aspect of a Memory Palace, however, is the chamber—the defined space indoors or out that sequesters one set of activities from another, one set of ideas from another. Rooms and courts, the chambers in architecture, help us sort. They come in various shapes and sizes and are more and less confining in the uses they encourage and/or allow. Great rooms ennoble gatherings; intimate ones shelter precious moments. Stern cloisters imprint order on the mind, lush patios harbor its secrets. The powder room isolates activities unthinkable in the dining room, the foyer offers the space (or time) to manage the transition from being outside to being inside, to shift garments if necessary, and to prepare the mind for a new encounter.

Rooms and courts set up our expectations and are the cells that store our memories. To serve us well in this regard they must be carefully fashioned, shaped so that we can (and want to) remember them, sized to allow freedom of movement regardless of the activities intended, and sheltered from undesirable noises, smells, and distractions—from sensory phenomena inappropriate for or destructive to the cluster of thoughts and impressions being formed.

Not only the size of a room or its degree of enclosure are of consequence in determining its character, but the way the defining walls, floors, and ceiling are proportioned and the

Pembroke courtyard, Providence, Rhode Island

locations of openings within them. The clearest rooms are ones
with simple geometric figures: squares, rectangles, circles in
plan; cubes, parallelepipeds, and domed cylinders in volume. The
simplest doesn't always work, though—the inside of a pyramid
is likely to be less than satisfying, and few triangular rooms exist.

Generally, we like the walls of a room to be vertical—
to make something we can stand up to and measure. On the

other hand, the most satisfying rooms often have ceilings that in some way enfold. Domes, vaults, and sloped or coffered ceilings imply that they are shaped around the inhabitant within. To hold our affections rooms need to seem as though they've been made to hold us, or some heroic version of ourselves. That's where proportions and context come into play: broad low rooms may be high enough to give headroom and broad enough to contain the movement of many people, yet they are likely to feel squashed and cramped unless they are intended for only a few and are open to higher and broader spaces on their edges. In previous centuries big rooms to house many people were almost always high, if only to ensure an adequate volume of air for their inhabitants. With the advent of mechanized ventilation penny-wise builders reduced heights; producing, in recent decades, a plethora of foolish flat ballroom and terminal spaces that are adequately filled with oxygen, but are mentally suffocating.

A noble memorable room has immediately definable limits, a volume great enough to afford an appropriate freedom of action and bounding shapes that are carefully measured and related one to another. Such rooms, you may say, are like grand and exclusive categories: impressive, but dull. They are only dull if they do not sustain our attention. An empty room whose walls are well proportioned can be satisfyingly peaceful, evoking the sense of concordance that is familiar in music when notes of harmonious intervals are used. Surfaces that are subdivided by doors, windows, pilasters, and moldings into shapes that have a recurrent proportion or that are commensurate with each other can intrigue the measuring eye, leading it to register a persistent character; nervous and insistent if the proportions are attenuated vertically or horizontally and the dimensions are not varied; calming and secure if they approximate the golden mean; static if they are square. Many systems of proportion exist and are helpful—but not so exclusively that they are required; you can count on your eyes.

Most rooms do not remain empty, however, they serve instead as chambers that shelter our actions and the things we use and admire. Rooms most often become fascinating by virtue of what they hold—not just tables, lamps, and chairs but things of the mind; pictures, memorabilia, and equipment. Specially cherished furnishings and objects like your ancestors' portraits or my father's desk, a temple model from Bangkok or the butcher-block table in the Sea Ranch Condominium, nurture recollection. They bring forth, on call, thoughts about how they were made, to whom they belonged, or what they portend.

It's the very nature of a room, however, that it does not exist in a vacuum. Each room sets space apart from neighboring spaces, yet the proximities and sequences that are established by joining and separating rooms powerfully affects our perceptions of them. An especially interesting collection of rooms can be found in the Palazzo Ducale in Urbino. The range of sizes and shapes in the rooms of a palace this large is remarkable—sorting, as it did, the various types of interaction allowable between the numerous members of the duke's court and their encounters, in turn, with the townspeople. The sizes of the rooms, their patterns of interaction, and the subtleties of their configuration and detailing are all instructive.

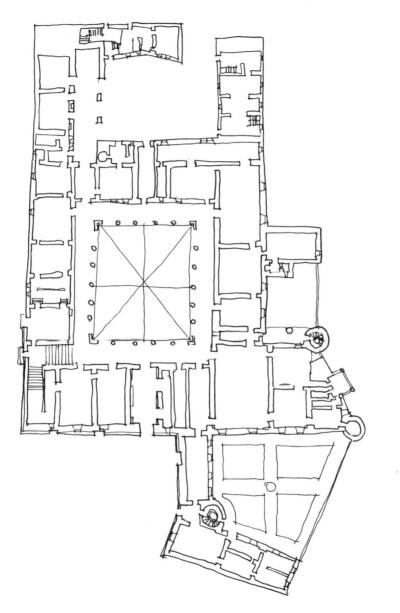

Palazzo Ducale, Urbino, Italy

The first and most surprising room is the forecourt previously mentioned that faces the town. Its borders are defined on two sides by walls embellished with a startlingly refined set of doors and windows. They create an ambiance that, while maintaining a clear and definable distinction between inside and out, is welcoming and stately in a manner that suggests that this plaza is in effect the first in the rooms of the palace.

Palazzo Ducale, Urbino, Italy

Entry to the main section of the palace is through one of the five apparent doors facing the plaza, into a vaulted foyer (which in turn had more door frames marked out along its length than were ever used, suggesting more openness than it allowed) and on into the famous arcaded courtyard. This is a wonderful clear space that is much noted in books on the architecture of the Renaissance as giving definitive form to the "problem" of an arcade on columns turning around the edges of a courtyard; the problem being that if the two intersecting walls of the corner land on one column, the regular rhythm of surfaces above the column is obliterated, making the corner seem unsteady. The "solution" here, and subsequently, was to make the corner a pier, giving it greater thickness and solidity. Here the visual strength of the pier is reinforced with a giant order pilaster, thereby making the four-cornered room of the court dominate over the continuous arcade around its perimeter.

Moving up into the palace, even the stair follows the format of distinct chambers, its two long runs divided by a solid wall and framed clearly at each end. At the second level a hall surrounds the courtyard, with openings paced to the arches below and rooms ranked around the outer edges of three sides, each connected to the next by a continuous line of doors. On the fourth side, nearest the stair, is the Great Hall, a single room roughly 45 feet wide and 105 feet long with a vaulted ceiling nearly 40 feet above. This huge room is lit by three large windows facing the plaza outside and is measured on the opposite face by arched entries at either end opening from the side passages of the corridor and by two very large fireplaces, paired with the entries. This clearly was the place of assembly inside the palace. It opened in turn to the throne room and the chambers reserved for the duchess.

The throne room, a mere 35 by 60 feet, is in many ways the most privileged room in the palace, located so that it has access from the Great Hall, from the corridor passage, from the row of rooms along the western edge of the court, and from the suite of private chambers reserved for the duke. Two large window openings provide outlook to the private gardens built over the stables. It has one large fireplace hood sporting an extraordinarily free, asymmetrical frieze of playful cherubs and is entered through inlaid wooden doors depicting perspective scenes of an ideal city.

Beyond this room, in the sequence, is a set of private rooms for the duke that can only be accessed from it, or from stairs twisting down into the lower chambers and service cellars, or up toward the towers. The duke's rooms include one that is nearly square, and a cluster of small, erratic, and irregular niches and chambers that result from the intersection of this great rectangular organization with the angled slope of the hillside and a great wall twisted out to follow the contours more closely. In these small chambers are lodged a cluster of curious chapels and the renowned Studiolo, an irregular space lined with inlaid wooden panels representing in astonishing perspective the array of instruments, tools, books, and images pertinent to princely culture when Federico da Montefeltro was duke and a patron for the blossoming of the Renaissance.

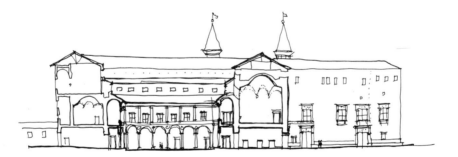

Palazzo, Ducale, Urbino, Italy

Beyond this chamber still, and outside the wall, is an elegant balcony bracketed between the twin turrets of the castle, with a coffered vault above, pilasters measuring the wall behind, and two elegant columns at the outer edges framing the view. It

Palazzo Ducale, Urbino, Italy

must have been satisfying indeed for Montefeltro to stand on
this balcony, facing the road to Rome (expecting, no doubt
either homage or money) with, behind his head, a set of cham-
bered rooms containing images, memories, and lessons of the
world he knew—and, to a great extent, controlled.

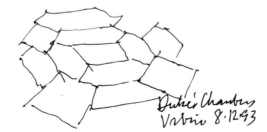

Palazzo Ducale, Urbino, Italy

Palazzo Ducale, Urbino, Italy

• DEAR DONLYN, Yet another way to make a room fascinating, which is my favorite, is to alter the borders, to blow out some of the walls, ceiling, or the floor, or—and especially—the corners, to give us the chance to make the space inside escape, around the corners and out of sight, or down into the dark, or most expansively up into the light. It is here that we can begin to note that the space of architects is not quite like that of philosophers, nor of musicians, or national expansionists. Architects' space, most importantly, is the stuff of which architecture is made. It is a substance capable of being closely held or manipulated, or set free to vanish around a corner. It is not empty nothingness, but more like what the Chinese call *chi,* which means something between space and spirit. In Chinese paintings of some periods, the spaces are called *lung mo,* or dragon's veins, which perhaps more vividly suggests the simultaneous emphasis and energy valued by the painter or acupuncturist, or the urban planner for whom the critical spaces are lungs that nurture the rest.

    The first large interior space of importance in the history of architecture is the Roman Pantheon, which is indeed interior, but with a hole opened out the top for light and to make the sizable space come alive. One of my favorite spaces of the nineteenth century, which makes a nice foil to that, is the breakfast room in Sir John Soane's house in London, a small room that seems grand. Its four walls continue past the ceiling, a handkerchief dome suspended clear of the walls, so that they slide out of view up into a skylit space, with pictures hung on the walls so they disappear up into the light, whose source is not revealed. A little lantern in the dome reveals while it falsifies the actual source of light. The light is almost never bright on that dark London street, but the unexpected glow, deep in the dim interior of the row houses, is truly magic.

I suppose the most stunning collections of rooms exploded in light that the world affords come from eighteenth-century Germany and Italy. In Rome the Bibiena brothers etched designs of dazzling drama, whose space seems to float

Pantheon, Rome, Italy

Sir John Soane's House, London

209

off the floor and up into a boundless upper world. The prison etchings of Gian Battista Piranesi develop the same compelling theme, but here, generally, the foreground, gloomily a place of suffering, is cut off from physical access to the liberating spaces above in the light. The freedom of light is made more poignant by its denial. But gravity was a more ardent disciplinarian on

Prison etching (after Piranesi)

the architects than on the illustrators, and few buildings soared
so grandly as the Bibiena and Piranesi illustrations.

A few did: The little parish church in Die Wies, previously mentioned, is on a sunny day a symphony of space that
soars into light. A double-cased elliptical nave looks into a triple-
bay sanctuary, which itself comes off as a vaulted central space

flanked by pierced double-layered walls. In the nave, the inner ring is made of paired columns, with that small vertical ridge mentioned before, which tweaks the light as it passes out of the sun causing it to be suddenly at its very brightest, just before the darkest patch of shade ensues.

But I've written earlier about the light. The main point here is that the space, made by tearing out part of the walls, is

Parish church in Die Wies, Germany

not fixed in light; it comes alive in light, and then dissolves as it goes up into the painted infinities of the sky, with golden hosts.

Wies, a magnificently charged burst of spatial energy, has some contemporaries that strike other spatial grace notes. Neresheim's painted interior columns stand free of the walls, on bases higher than a human head, so the grand white columns seem to glow and to start beyond our grasp, and head up into another world, light and free like the upper reaches of the Piranesi prisons.

The spatial fantasies of the Bibienas show up almost as aerially in a number of palaces in Genoa, where entrance typically is on a lower street, into a grand stair hall with passages up, then on up the hill into courtyards in the sky. The movement up into the light is more memorable even than the most flamboyant details that grace the palazzi.

Even more recently, there is the curious case of the atrium hotels and office buildings that had caused a stir early in the twentieth century, when elevators first made multiple stories practical, and such proud hostelries as the Brown Palace Hotel in Denver sported a spacious atrium, which promoted a sense of grandeur. Then the hotel industry shifted the emphasis to a more constrained efficiency, and ceilings got low and flat. John Portman broke that mold in 1957 with the Hyatt Regency in Atlanta, with its twenty-two story atrium up through which ride glass elevators with sparkling lights. The novel space was an instant success; critics noted the "Jesus Christ spot" where two steps inside the atrium the tired businessman, his eyes on the floor, would catch the glimmer of a rising elevator, look up, murmur "Jee-sus Christ," and drop his briefcase. Architecture as experience, after a brief absence, was back in the public eye.

Court house · St. George · Utah.
CUMROKO

St. George, Utah

COMPOSITIONS *Types that Recur / Order that Comes and Goes*

 *The recurrence of familiar themes and types of spatial organization aid in the ordering of places. For some time now, order has been simplemindedly found in such acts as lining up the heads of windows and doors, or in making regular modules in the plan. Such acts are not wicked but don't, it seems to us, constitute order. The order of things should reward our attention, not demand it. Patterns that are too obvious and insistent impose themselves upon our appreciation of a place rather than giving us the opportunity to find a subtler understanding. The natural world has much to teach us about order—not of the repetitive and ultimately boring simple sort, but of the complexly interactive sort that we live within. Some mathematicians and physicists are these days understanding the world better through a study of chaos, which turns out to be a subtler and nonrecurring kind of order.*

DEAR CHARLES, All the foregoing Memory Chambers are built around specific ways of organizing space and form, evoking an attachment to the characteristics of a specific place. We should turn our attention now to relationships that give structure to a whole place and help us to hold it in the mind.

Underlying all other observations and perceptions about places are generic clusters of organization that establish the most fundamental basis for our reactions and expectations—clusters of elements that, when arranged in certain ways, tell us that it is one kind of place or another: a castle or a church, a dwelling or a warehouse, a highway or a promenade. These clusters of relationships, referred to usually as types, come about through customary usage, through our experience, over and over again, of the same sets of relationships in the same sort of order serving the same sets of uses. Ramparts surrounding a clutch of buildings with protective gates and towers make a castle type; a dominant main hall preceded by ceremonial entry spaces and marked by a tower with a cross signals a church.

The elements that come together to form a type vary with the building's purpose and the character of the culture that developed the pattern, but generally types combine a particular way of accessing and moving through the structure with a characteristic pattern of room sizes and proximities and a distinctive volume and silhouette. The court house in its square is a public type common in many regions of the country. There are several

Single family and row house types

dwelling types, their differences derived from the amount of
space commonly afforded to a family, the characteristics of the
climate in which they are found, and the density of the dwelling settlement for which they are intended. A free-standing
single-family house, of the sort built so ubiquitously throughout
the towns of the United States that they can be called to mind
by a simple cartoon, consists of a front and a back porch, a set
of varied rooms accessed from them, taking advantage from
light on all sides, often arranged on more than one level, and
with a roof silhouette generally centered on the mass of the
house in a peak or a ridge. A city-dwelling row house, on the
other hand, is typified by an entry porch that leads to a hall and
stair on one side with a narrow stack of rooms beside it, garner-
ing light only from the front and back (and sometimes a light
shaft in the middle) and with an indeterminate roof, which
influences the house form far less than the walls—unless it is
combined with that of its neighbors in large roofs that encompass many houses at once. The warehouse, as a type, is dominated by its size, large openings for moving goods in and out,

and undifferentiated spaces and windows; the construction system (wood and masonry, steel frame or concrete) tends to determine its specific character. The barn, likewise, has several generic types related to regional customs of construction, yet in any one place the basic type may be modified to suit the slope, the microclimate, or particular uses.

Types have the power to lend weight to our perceptions, confirming and amplifying our experience of a place by lending it a substratum of recollection and familiarity. Modernists, confident of their ability to invent a new and better world,

Barns, Anderson Valley, California

have been hostile to types, seeing them as the embodiment of unexamined habits and ossified relationships, as impediments to the creation of forms and spaces that would afford new experiences and capitalize on the possibilities offered by changes in technology and social organization. Others, bedazzled by the pace of change, and dismayed by some of the fruits of modern invention, look to the codification of types as a brake on change, a guide to the making of things that incorporate a form of collective wisdom—tried and true. Some go so far as to attribute to traditional types a form of cultural memory, invoking for types of spatial organization an authority that bears no tolerance of change.

For our part it seems more plausible to acknowledge that the recurrence of certain types of organization does have mnemonic power, which we can tap or forego, depending on the circumstances at hand. The usefulness of familiarity depends on the purposes to which the place is to be put. Feeling at home in a place is more often useful than not; it is often a boon to be able to work within patterns that have proven over time to be workable. Saving our energies for crucial bits of inventive modification is often more humanly productive than tilting at the windmills of social and economic organization.

The advantage to the modification of traditional types is that they have developed, usually, in response to a complex of forces. They represent a fusion of many different concerns. Even as they are altered and adjusted to give unaccustomed weight to one factor, or to meet special circumstances of site, they retain a connection to the fused network of considerations that made them whole. Judicious use and modification of established types guards against the creation of buildings that are single-minded. Outright replication of a type, on the other hand, is simplistic; almost always a freshening is in order—adjustments to the site, unexpected combinations of subsidiary elements, an incompleteness in the pattern, or an addition to the volume—jostling the pattern just enough to awaken its evocative power and open new opportunities.

Types, like geometric patterns and other ordering devices, should be the starting point, not the goal, of the architect's activities. The mental order embodied in buildings is there for inhabitants to find and use to their advantage. It should be discovered by its users, not imposed upon them. Unfortunately the buildings of our world now seem to totter between being carelessly incomprehensible or brutally dominant, characterized by a simplistic idea, bluntly proclaimed and mindlessly insistent. They would seem to say that we must choose between inchoate jumbles of construction and an abstracted cerebral architecture that is indifferent to human experience.

Lou Kahn's geometries come so readily to mind when thinking either of the insistence of order or of the profundities of its distortion that inevitably they must be discussed. Kahn's geometries, of course, derived from the pure self-regulating forms of the classical tradition, transmitted through his Beaux-Arts training and invested with the intellectual heritage of neoplatonism; rational clarity as an ideal, inherent within (but inaccessible to) the imperfect world of everyday appearances. His building for the I. M. Richards Medical Center at the University of Pennsylvania in Philadelphia is the first for which he fully proclaimed his compelling distinction between "served" and "servant" spaces; distinguishing a hierarchy between those spaces that house the principal activities of the building and those, like mechanical chases, closets, and toilets, which are

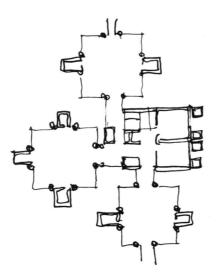

I.M. Richards Medical Center, Philadelphia, Pennsylvania

subservient in character or separable from the experience of the place. The servant spaces here, and in later buildings, were then used as elements to define the larger structure of the place, elements that derived their meaning not from what was housed within them, but from their position in the larger assembly. In the Richards Building, servant spaces were placed outside the periphery of clear-span studio spaces designated for laboratory work. In subsequent buildings there was a continual elaboration of these distinctions, providing in each case for a classification of room types, then assembling the larger and smaller spaces in patterns of mutual dependence, each with a predictable location in the larger whole.

In the Salk Institute at La Jolla, some years later, the pattern almost reverses itself: the large, adaptable, and contingent laboratory spaces become the background to columns of studies that stand free along their sides, the smaller spaces carrying the figural importance in the composition, signaling the creative force of individual study set against the instrumental, confirming role of laboratory experimentation. Here, and at the Richards Building, much of the power of the place comes from the classification of spaces and their formation into the elements from which the building is forged, each in an allotted place within a comprehensible diagram. For the assembly building that was originally projected to be a part of the Salk complex, Kahn made what has always been, for me, his most compelling diagram; the rooms clustered in a hierarchical square, about a

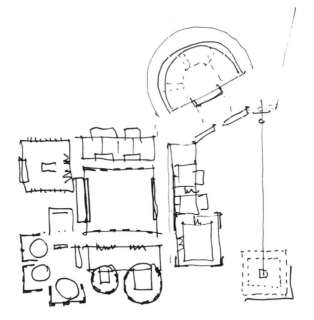

Salk Research Institute Assembly Building, La Jolla, California

communal center, with each of the corners made differently to accommodate differing uses and outlook; each room shaped at once by its position in the topological figure, by the freedom of its unbounded edges, and by the character of an intended use. It suggests an order that lends import without demanding simplistic geometric compliance.

• DEAR DONLYN, For me, one of Lou Kahn's most compelling studies in the byways of order is the Goldenberg house, which studies a far different balance between the general and specific situation at each point, so that it makes out of simple pieces a far more varied and intricate order that transcends the order of a mere immediate response. I remember once hear-

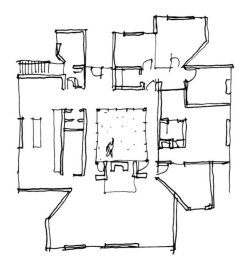

Goldenberg House, plan

ing Kahn describe the orderly impulses that organized the Goldenberg house, framing each rafter directly to the size and shape
of the space it spans, but with a connection still to the order
and framing of the whole house. That, in turn, reminded me of
our mentor George Rowley's comparison of Chinese and Western art, the latter represented by the figure of a human body,
symmetrical, its power coming from within, the former by
shoots of bamboo, where the external circumstance, the sun and
wind and air, have much more to do with the particular shape
portrayed, though the essential bamboo is not diminished. Isn't
that Goldenberg house more like the bamboo—and isn't that
less diagrammatic order somehow connected to the recent physical and mathematical studies of chaos reported by Gleick
(*Chaos,* 1988), which describe the realization that the disorders
and discontinuity that mathematicians have tried to suppress and
physicists have ascribed to cheap equipment bought from stingy
grants are not glitches, but a subtler, nonrepetitive part of order.
There are illustrations in Gleick's book of fractal geometries and
plottings of chaos that look a lot like the paintings and especially architecture of people like Alvar Aalto, whom I admired
even in my school days, when "order" was so ardently sought
but was so casually linked in students' minds with flat-footed
acts like lining up the door heads. I had admired Aalto's interest
in the specific, in shapes that resulted from deformation of the
ideas and then from enjoying the deformation, exulting in it.
He did not try, as most of his contemporaries did, to deny the
differences and to find similarities in almost equal components,
to glory in order and banish strangeness, but instead to take
strangeness in stride. A case in point is a collection of

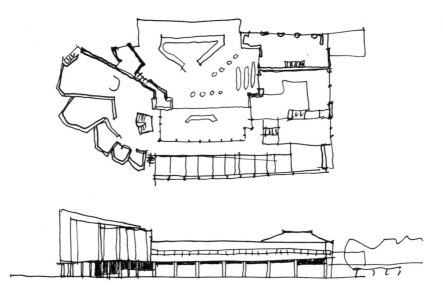

Wolfsburg Cultural Center, Germany

second-story lecture rooms in the Cultural Center in
Wolfsburg, Germany, in which the shapes expand, progressively,
enjoying their difference while not forgetting their sameness.
The columns beneath them, following the expanding edge, to-
tally transform the rhythm of a simple colonnade. It's chaos theory prefigured.

Ornamental forms

COMPOSITIONS Shapes that Remind / Ornament that Transmits, Transforms, and Encodes

This century started with the ringing slogan that ornament is a crime. Decades later, its absence was much regretted. Layers of expressive detail on a building identify the culture of the place where it is built and the conditions of its making. Ornament clarifies the voice of the structure, indicates its position in the society, and rewards our attention. The most valuable ornament does not simply transmit tradition, but transforms our expectations. Certain shapes have become so embedded in our culture that they carry with them recollections that bind us together.

D E A R   C H A R L E S ,   The fractal geometries that you refer to as a more complex kind of order lead our minds to forces external to the building, beyond our realm of influence. The simpler, self-referencing forms of Euclidean geometry turn the mind inward to the discovery of consistencies, hierarchies, and centers, to constructs of self-regulated thought. The Euclidean geometries may be most useful in developing a memorable structure that can be replicated—as a Memory Palace must be. Complex geometries carry greater differentiating force, creating patterns that are vividly unique, capable of causing memories and associations to adhere to them and to be brought back to mind by their utter particularity.

There are also some generic shapes that are so deeply embedded in our culture that they almost inevitably start a train of associations, reminding us of other places, other cultures, or, more simply, the presence of other people. To carry such associative force, these shapes must in turn be either ubiquitous—found again and again so that they become thoroughly familiar—or so intensely, so engagingly particular that they are emblazoned in our minds. The gable roof typifies the former, the Eiffel Tower may stand in for the latter.

The gable roof with its peak along the spine is so generic that it is found in all cultures that build with wood. Its shape is inherent to the process of building with pieces of wood sloping toward each other for mutual support to span a roof.

Church tower, Italy

Unadorned and large, the gable makes most Americans think
"barn"; in the reductive scrawl of cartoons it means "house."
Set on a real house, with a projecting eave and Classically derived moldings, the gable is integral to the conception of a
Greek Revival house, intended, in early nineteenth-century
America, to remind home builders and citizens, often building
on the edge of wilderness west of the Appalachians, of their

connection to the political and cultural verities formulated in Greece and passed on through the secular traditions of Europe to the fledgling United States.

The triangular end piece of a gable, codified initially in the megarons of Greece and celebrated subsequently with the refinements of a Classical pediment, has an extraordinarily wide symbolic usage. It appears in many guises throughout Western architecture: in the ends of major and minor roof forms, over dormers, windows, porches, and doors, occasionally even inside. A pediment reminds simultaneously of the Classical tradition (however vaguely) and of the implicit presence of people. In its most primitive form it used to signal the throne of the chieftain, as you pointed out in Roofs that Encompass. With its implicit

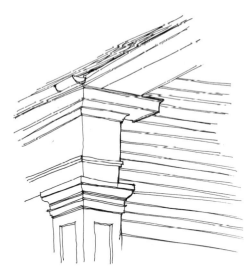

Wooden gable roof detail, Michigan

Pedimented doorway

centering, the pediment remains (in any mildly literate
work) associated with entries,
its size gauging importance;
or with places where people
gather or that they come to for
outlook, like porches, bays, and
dormers. The gable and pediment forms can retain their
value in current work because
they do not merely simulate
previous forms, but have an inherent logic related to the acts
of building and to our uses of

them. Shapes that remind are only really effective when they
also serve a current purpose, providing both recollection and
present experience.

You will object, Charles, that my discussion of Shapes
that Remind is altogether too confined; that there are many,
many examples throughout architecture where the primary organizing ideas for the building were based on the recall of prior
places and times—from the inchoate but profoundly moving
and evocative recollections of the Roman past in Romanesque
architecture to more trivially motivated current exercises in association. The search for the exotic that created many of the most
endearing of nineteenth-century monuments and mansions was
often pursued with an exuberance that caused the parvenus to
outreach their mentors. The Wagnerian castle built by "Mad
Ludwig" at Neuschwanstein comes to mind, or the Tuscan re-

House, Marshall, Michigan

vival villas in New England, or that marvelously exuberant
house in Marshall, Michigan, that is meant to be Hawaiian.
Whatever these places did for their owners, they remind us still
of the extraordinary aspirations of their builders, and one cannot
but admire their strength of will. In each of these examples,
though, the remembrances are not thin; they each are buildings
composed in depth. Neuschwanstein was elaborated with the
aid of an army of craftsmen, the "Tuscan villas" were transformed to meet the demands of the climate, the house in Marshall was encoded by an extraordinary array of carved sticks.

    The house in Atlantic City, New Jersey, that photo-
graphs show to be shaped like an elephant presumably had
fewer redeeming qualities. Perhaps, though, its insides had some
of the marvelous qualities of the inside of the Statue of Liberty,
where all those folds of the drapery, when seen in segments
from the inside—inside out and juxtaposed against the vigorous
supporting framework designed by Gustave Eiffel—make a truly
astounding and memorable experience, one that adds distinct

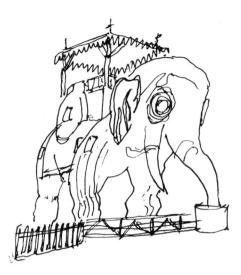

Elephant House, Atlantic City, New Jersey

personal attachment to a symbolic structure that is otherwise thoroughly codified.

Not coincidentally, Eiffel's Tower in Paris provides a similar mix of the iconic shape and extraordinary experience. The trusswork of its structure creates an enveloping web of steel against the sky as you move up and through one of its capacious legs. Several artists of the period attempted to capture the thrill of moving through such an elaborate structure, a structure that loomed far higher in the sky than anyone had previously encountered, but which in the end was made just to be experienced and remembered. The sinuous curves of its legs as they come to the ground and the great arches binding them together in triumph are a marvel, not only of engineering, but of the crafting of form. The exposed struts, bolts, and angles of its detailed structure may seem utilitarian, but the inherent folly of its

existence belies the designation, and the array of stairs, platforms, and elevators winding its way up through the structure
to its apex provides a kinetic experience without parallel in
scope and intensity, short of the wonders of an amusement park.

In this case, though, the amusements of a complex personal experience are linked to a form that can be seen from anywhere in the city. As Roland Barthes has pointed out, this leads

Eiffel Tower, Paris, France

to a very particular fusion of remembrances for anyone who has
been to the top, a curious mutuality of associations—from the
top of the tower you can see all of central Paris, identifying
from a new vantage point places that are familiar in everyday
experience; conversely, from anywhere in the city that you can
see the Tower you may be reminded of being at its top,

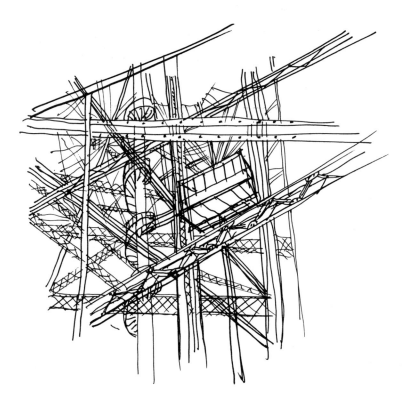

Eiffel Tower, Paris, France

figuratively transformed into an overseer. To the suitably imaginative, the Tower allows a simultaneity of detachment and engagement, a state of mind as peculiarly modern, perhaps, as the structure itself.

The act of imagining yourself into a place such as the top of the Eiffel Tower is an act that is central to the power that architecture has to remind us of things, events, and other places. We understand places by inhabiting them vicariously, imagining what it would be like to look out a certain window or to stand in a porch or to move freely through a large unencumbered space. We match the appearance of a building or a piece of building with our remembered experience of it, or something like it. We do this all the time—without the recollections that similarities provide, we would hardly know how to behave in a new place. The shapes of doors and windows and furniture remind us how to use them, the configuration of a building type sets up our expectations for what will be done inside, the character of a street or place helps us remember a whole district, the decor of a room reminds us to act with

View to Campidoglio from Roman Forum, Rome, Italy

suitable decorum. In Memory Palaces, especially those of the Jesuits of the seventeenth century, the sequence and pattern of spaces sorted and classified ideas, but it was the shapes of particular objects that reminded.

●   D E A R   D O N L Y N ,   Maybe the most manipulable—and therefore for the architect the most important—aspect of Shapes that Remind is ornament: the whole system of shapes and patterns that helps buildings speak and that frames the speech in a manner that contributes to our understanding of what they're talking about.

      Ornament got off to a bad start in this century with the Viennese Adolf Loos's published assertion that "ornament is crime," based presumably on the high-flown decoration (less integral than ornament, more superficially applied) that was triumphant in Franz Josef's Vienna. The result for modern architecture was that ornament went into hiding; it changed its scale so that, for instance, a whole small building might with a striking shape become an ornament, like Le Corbusier's Villa

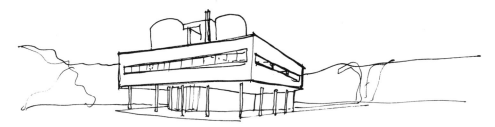

Villa Savoye, Poissy, France

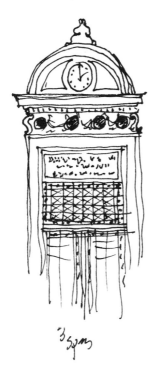

245

Doe Library, UC Berkeley, California

Savoye, or ornament might simply be expunged as on most modern buildings, which leaves more than ample opportunity for random cracks and uninhibited weathering to play an important if unplanned part in what the eyes see.

But ornament speaks of many things, including the people who designed the building and the people for whom it was designed. And occasionally, as in Classical times, it spoke in tones so fully agreed on that the message became clear and explicit. Take the previously mentioned Classical orders of architecture. Doric, it was agreed, was steadfast and sturdy, its proportions based on the male body with no frills and careful agreement about the unadorned parts (no articulating, for instance, between the column and the floor) and the swell of the simple parts that are there (like the abacus at the top of the column or the swell of the column itself), to make some connection with the feel of muscles performing the task of supporting the loads.

Or there is the Ionic order, slender and more feminine, adorned for instance at the base of the columns where Doric is bare. The volutes at the capital, primly voluptuous, and finely wrought moldings like the egg and dart with suggestions of fer-

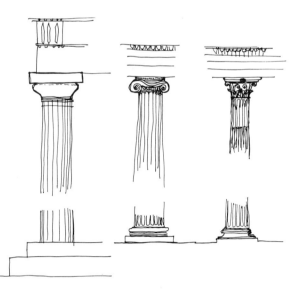

Diagrams of capitals and bases, three orders

tility differentiate the Ionic from the robust Doric, but like it were perfected over hundreds of years, a development unparalleled in the history of Western architecture toward complete agreement about all the details.

The third classical order, the Corinthian, was developed, the old story ran, because acanthus leaves in Corinth crept over a basket at a child's grave, suggesting to designers a much fuller, more decorative, and more unabashedly or floridly monumental order than either the Doric or Ionic, and instituting a format for structures more fancy and more complex than the first two. The role that choice has in clarifying the content of architecture is fascinating: with the choice of Doric, Ionic, or

Ornament, S. Andrea al Quirinale, Rome, Italy

Corinthian ornament (and afterward the Tuscan and Composite), each with a fully worked-out grammar and vocabulary, there is the chance to refine the message with restrictions but with considerable precision. Less familiar in the West is the Japanese choice between *wabi* (pure), *sabi* (rustic), and *iki* (flamboyant). It is not bad taste (ugh) and good taste (whoopee)—it is three alternative tastes (all okay). You take your pick.

But the twentieth century in the West has some real choices too: Antonio Gaudi in Barcelona devised his own plastic ornament, based on some astonishing local work of a period

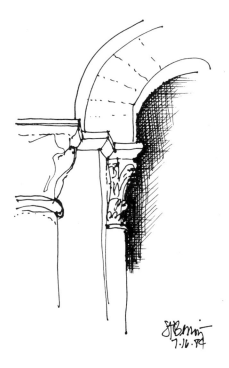

Pier, St. Benoit sur Loire, France

Palace of Fine Arts, San Francisco, California

just before him, which is so friendly to the elements that the surface on his capitals at Casa Batllo, for instance, becomes clearer and stronger as it weathers, like good late Gothic work where rain and soot enhance highlight and shadow. And on Bernard Maybeck's 1915 Palace of Fine Arts in San Francisco, hooded figures create another kind of shadow, one of mood, turning their faces to the building and their backs to the visitor. As we've mentioned, even Mies van der Rohe, working in the very mainstream of ornamentless modern architecture, planted five-inch I-beams on apartment facades whose own steel structural I-beams were, by law, buried under concrete fireproofing, in order to talk about how the buildings were made.

Gothic (and Gothic revival) builders so loved the shapes with which they dealt, pointed arches and pointed frames, that they used them when they got the chance on ornament, on aedicular homes for the saints, or even Gothic chair backs. Rococo stuccoteurs extended their curvilinear forms from saints to column capitals and views of the heavens. Long before them Egyptian painters had extended with pigment the world their sculptors had chiseled from hard stone.

Ornament, then, through human history has transmitted the artists' and architects' vision of their world, as it has transformed the vision into abstractions that reinforce the shape of buildings and their component parts and encode the messages they care about transmitting. Whether these parts follow the water of the roof through gargoyles and into downspouts or divide walls into imaginable pilastered segments—and the visions are of heaven or hell or of both at once—ornament extends the power of buildings to hold our thoughts.

Garden speculations

12 GARDENS THAT CIVILIZE

 *Paradise, as everyone knows, was a garden, and generally still is. When Adam and Eve were in a state of grace, their garden provided both shelter and nourishment. But in the harsher times since, people have progressed to a level of sufficiency that lets them build houses and grow food long before they arrive at that higher state that gives them the leisure to build gardens for their pleasure. Buildings are vessels into which human energy can pour. When they have enough, they begin to pay it back in satisfaction to the occupants. Gardens require even more energy, continuously given, for a garden soon disappears without ongoing care. But the pleasures it gives back are perhaps the most precious of all, in sheer delight and in the sense of being connected to the earth, and all the natural world.*

DEAR CHARLES, It's funny how the Salk Institute lurks in the memory, whether or not one intends it to. It comes to mind again when we speak of gardens—albeit somewhat ruefully. When I first visited Salk it was just being completed, and I wrote about it then, enthusiastically, summing up with a description of the stacked office clusters bracketing the central open space "waiting for the garden to grow." The garden in question was one that I was then told was planned for the space between the two buildings. I don't remember that I had seen a plan for the garden, but somehow I had imagined it would be a fragrant oasis, akin probably to the sacred playgrounds of Krishna found in Indian paintings. That space, of course, became instead the famous paved court opening baldly, some say cosmically, to a stunning view of the ocean to the west.

The court, as it finally came to be, is a bare, bright, hard surface of travertine paving blocks, screened at one end by a thicket of Monterey pine, open at the other to the ocean's horizon. It is split down the middle by a narrow channel of water and animated only by the stalking shadows of the columnar office towers and by the occasional passing of white-coated workers, their deliberate pace syncopated to skip across the shallow chasm. The space, as it is, is a far cry from what I had imagined, but it is arguably a garden still: a controlled space open to the air, bounded so that experience is set to measure and sequestered sufficiently to nurture reflection and enjoyment.

Gardens come in all shapes and sizes, from the most intimate and personal to the most public and sublime, and with every conceivable level of sophistication in design, execution, and maintenance. They merit attention especially because they are so thoroughly invested with care, and more linked to the elements and cycles of nature than most buildings are. Gardens remain gardens only with effort; bereft of attention they decay (as indeed do buildings, though generally at a slower pace).

Most interesting, though, is the capacity gardens have to civilize, a capacity to mediate between nature and humankind. The fascinating thing is that gardens create a middle ground that can work both ways: gardens in the wilderness are evidence of human control; a garden in the midst of buildings reasserts nature's presence. At Salk it does so by turning atten-

Salk Research Institute, La Jolla, California

tion starkly to the sea, the sky, and the course of the sun. On the other hand, in the enclosed garden courtyard of the Isabella Stewart Gardner Museum in Boston, which you mentioned earlier, nature is served up delicately, as though on a tray; rendering more of Venice than of the landscape of the Veneto, and virtually nothing of Boston's intemperate climate or of the Fens in which it is built.

The garden for my house at the Sea Ranch, on the other hand, is going to be based, quite simply, on domesticating the little drainage swale that passes through our lot. We will enclose a bit of it (square, like paradise, of course) in a high stake fence to separate it from the larger, deliberately unkempt landscape, then thin out enough of the swamp grass to make room for the water to pool, for native azaleas to prosper, and perhaps for a few roses to bloom in secret splendor. I'm sure that before it's done Alice will have set some inscribed granite inside it and that somewhere there'll be a hollowed stone to assemble whatever droplets of moisture descend from the air. Mostly it will be sequestered, a small part of the land set apart and subjected to our will —but only a small part, even of our small lot, and not visible to others except as a fence. The larger rural landscape pattern that is the basis for the Sea Ranch will carry through— unless, of course, my neighbor culverts the stream.

Builders of the great gardens like Versailles hardly needed to worry about the neighbors; nor, conversely, do the conventional caretakers of urban backyard gardens. In the era of royal gardens great tracts of land could be enclosed to supply ample scenery suitable for aristocratic pleasures. Axes and paths cut through the woodside, rows of statues, benches, and urns

and an army of tree-clipping, path-raking servants secured a seg-
ment of nature and transformed it into a place that would exem-
plify societal control. That these and similarly extravagant
gardens of the rulers retain a fundamentally civilizing role, even
as political structures have changed, is evident in the great care
that is lavished on most of them still—in Europe, Russia, and
Asia—long after their initial patronage has been dismantled and
some latter-day versions of "the people" prevail. To walk freely
in the open air, without hazard or nuisance, accompanied by
comforting signs that others have cared for and will continue to
care for the place is, it would seem, a near universal aspiration.
And why not?

The original garden suburbs were nearly such a dream,
projecting a garden of carriageways and common foliage, albeit
less manicured, with the additional feature that each family had
a territory of its own, nestled within the whole and privately
maintained. The garden suburb that has evolved in recent years
makes a mockery of the analogy, its paths given over to automo-
biles, their boundaries measured by garage doors, the foliage
picked to be maintenance-free, the front yards codified to a
numbing neutrality while the back yards, where they exist in
any size, remain as remnants of private initiative—pockets
where sufficient imagination may still civilize a few, but which
offer little scope for improving the public domain.

• DEAR DONLYN, Your words on gardens are, I think,
indisputable, and I like the way you open up the category, including places like the Salk courtyard. But a dimension, still, is

missing from the description, or maybe two—the one philo-
sophical, the other sensual. The first might well be addressed in
Ryoanji, in Kyoto, Japan, a Zen garden of fifteen rocks in a rectangular, raked gravel bed the size of a tennis court, and the latter might be noted at Saihoji, a moss garden nearby in Kyoto,
which plays on the senses.

      Ryoanji is an astonishment to Westerners who think of
a garden in terms of flowers, of which it has none, only fifteen
rocks arranged on a rectangle of sand with a porch on one side
to view the rectangle and the rocks and a gorgeously weathered
plaster wall behind, backed by a thick forest with a mossy
stretch around the corner. The garden as is is very old—500
years—but it was preceded on this site by a cherry orchard, so
it must have come about over time. The mica chips, sized between sand and gravel, are importantly raked around the rocks
to look like waves, so the visitors can see rocks and a bed of

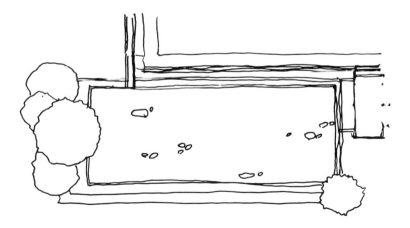

Ryoanji, Kyoto, Japan

Saihoji, Kyoto, Japan

sand or islands in the sea, or a story about a mother bear and her cubs crossing a stream, or a diagram of fixed points in the cosmos. It's a sort of divine map—a miniature—with the scale left up to the viewer and the meaning (if there is one) only to come clearer after a patient search.

Saihoji, nearby, is also the product of utter simplification and intensification meant, like Ryoanji, not to be touched. Saihoji is a reach of forest and lake and rocks with a sensual surface of soft green moss that covers everything, trunks and rocks and forest floor: One of the astonishments of this garden comes in reading descriptions of it. It turns out that what seems now the most utterly calm and composed garden on earth, perfectly balanced and at peace, was once famed for the ferocious activity it described. The rocks in a part of it were celebrated long ago in the power with which they suggested boulders tossed about by a raging torrent. It's hard to spot the tearing rage now, covered as always by the furry emerald moss and the dim and dappled porous light.

• DEAR CHARLES, Now you have left out what at least in the West is a major function of gardens—to record a level of civilization that has eluded most cultures and that shows up at special times and places in circumstances that are not about the provision of shelter or sustenance, but celebrate the power of the civilization to care about things beyond that. In a sense, that's what your Japanese gardens do, but the world is full of very different traditions that do it too, like Italian gardens (how about the Villa Lante?) or Spanish ones (like the Alhambra) But then, you have described those in the *Poetics of Gardens*.

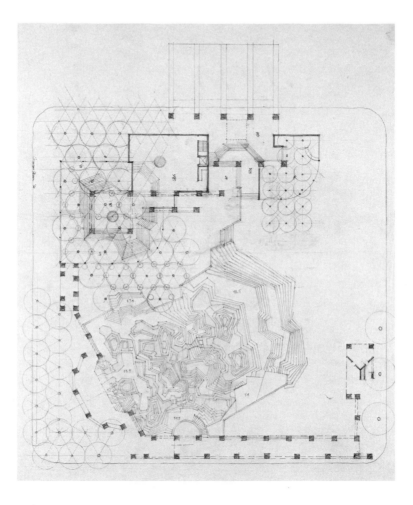

Plaza project, Portland, Oregon

13 WATER THAT POOLS AND CONNECTS

COMPOSITIONS Water that Pools and Connects

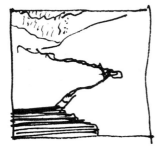

Water, a commonplace in our lives, has one extraordinary quality: all of it, everywhere, is connected symbolically and poetically with all the rest of the water on earth, some of it near, but some of it very far away in mysterious submarine depths. Moving, it can represent life, still, it can signify death—from the amniotic fluid to the waters of Styx. Its circulation on the earth is paralleled by the circulation of fluids in our bodies. Captured in pools and reflecting light, its cooling presence connects the infinite and the intimate.

C o m p o s i t i o n s   *Water that Pools and Connects*

• DEAR DONLYN, After a bout of soul searching I picked Water in Architecture as a topic for my Ph.D. dissertation. The year was 1956, the president Eisenhower, the mood matter-of-fact. Water as architectural material was exuberantly out of step with the times, possessed of mysterious qualities that relate, for instance, the water in a specific place with all the rest of the water in the world, so that a stream in the English Cotswolds maintains connections with the sea, ships, and mermaids and the fantastic and the forgotten. There is a story from sixteenth-century Japan of a garden for the tea ceremony on the shore of the inland sea, at a place where it was particularly rocky and magnificent. The garden's wall shut off the view of the sea except in one place—a small opening over the bowl where one bowed to wash one's face. There, when the bowl of water reflected the face and a glance outward showed the wild surf, the message was clear. The water of both was related to the life of the world.

Part of the mystery of water baffled humankind for almost all of history; how come it is always falling down out of the sky or down streams and waterfalls and into lakes and the sea? How does it get back up? Savants for millennia have had notions; Plato proposed a seesaw with water running down one way and then up the other. St. Augustine thought the water might climb to the mountain tops, seeking the stars. There are medieval drawings of water out beyond Gibraltar, in the unknown, whirling up into the sky. But none had seen water

Trevi Fountain, Rome, Italy

moving upward, and it was 1723 before Giovanni Poleni described the water cycle that we now learn about in junior high, including the evaporation that lifts water into the sky. The wonder is that with the mystery clarified the poetry got richer: the Trevi Fountain in Rome, the waterworks that set out to give form to the newly discovered water cycle, is surely the greatest, richest, most impressive, and most wondrous fountain yet devised.

Its main glory is the water falling in every manner possible—spouts, wiers, splashes—and finally at the bottom jetting into the air to help suggest the continuousness of the water cycle. The giant statue of Oceanus presides over it all, flanked by Abundance and Fertility and backed by a tablet showing a dancing Virgo, who showed Augustan soldiers the source in the suburbs of Rome of the Aqua Vergine that feeds the Trevi. Below Oceanus and his attendants there are sea horses, one wild and one tame, in the charge of tritons. The figures are of Carrara marble, white and smooth. The rocks and plants are travertine, smooth where the water is flowing, rough where it is not. At the bottom, sunken below the piazza, the water suggests the ocean with tide pools at its edge, from which spouts seek the heavens again. Here is water unabridged.

• DEAR CHARLES, The thing is, of course, that humans like their water abridged—that is to say, controlled and made to do their bidding (as it does in the pipes leading to the Trevi Fountain). In fact, we have so domesticated water that in most of the Western world we fully expect it to flow out of the walls and into our hands, hot, cold, or tepid, at any moment we choose and, with some less certainty, to flow off roads and sidewalks to vanish unheeded into the ground. In some dim way we know it takes an array of pipes, pumps, heaters, valves, and filters to do this, and that someone must watch over and care for the systems, but all that is not brought to mind except when roads flood, pipes leak, or nature refuses to cooperate—altering

The Seine, Paris, France

the supply uncontrollably through drought or rampaging downpour.

Waterworks have indeed been among the most ambitious of civilization's projects, dating from the earliest efforts to channel and exploit the flooding cycles of the Nile and Euphrates, emerging most visibly as majestic arcuated aqueducts stalking across the Roman Empire, embellishing, later, the public spaces of great cities and the sequestered gardens of Islamic palaces, and haunting our subterranean imagination in sinister descriptions of the Parisian sewer systems. For all their ingenuity all water systems depend on the simple proposition that water, domesticated or not, yearns for the sea. (More accurately, water, like everything else, seeks the center of the earth, but being slippery and mindless it shimmers across and around impervious material until it reaches its own in the ocean or in vast subterranean aquifers.) This gives it the endlessly subtle but generally predictable character that makes it such a potent and ubiquitous element of design—whether tracing through roof slope, gutter, and downspout, bubbling out of faucets and fountains, or shaping the slope of the land.

The most commonly visible forms of water control are channels of varying sorts; river banks, canals, raceways, pools, and ditches. My favorites are probably the banks of the Seine, passing through Paris in a mighty built cavern, its configuration bending gently in a marvelously poignant merging of the geometry of the mason with the sinuosity of water flow. At the opposite end of the scale I have never forgotten the tiny circular ditch formed in the mud flats behind the temple at Itsukushima in Japan, reminding one at once that the water will

Torii Gate, Itsikushima, Japan

return and that the mind is present. This wooden temple is, for my money, the most potent juxtaposition of frail but persistent human effort with the inexorable flow of water, manifest here in the tides of the Inland Sea. The great wooden torii gate, which you have previously mentioned, set out in the water at the limits of the tidal flat, is like an invitation to the sea—an invitation accepted each tidal cycle by the inflow of water rustling under the platforms of the temple, surrounding it at high tide in a lagoon, only to retreat again just beyond the toes of the gate.

I've never seen the elegantly spaced network of irrigation channels set into the pavement of the Patio of the Orange

Trees in Seville, but your description of them long ago left an indelible trace in my memory, a trace that surfaces whenever trees in hot urban places are called to mind. I suppose they must have been in the back of your thoughts, too, when you set that orchard of palm trees in a pond at the Oceanside Civic Center.

The intermediate-sized channel that I like the best is Cascade Charley, the one Alice Wingwall created for you in the Hatfield Science Center at the University of Oregon. The water, bubbling up quietly among granite slabs in a pool on an upper level, then flowing down a four foot channel beside the

Cascade Charley, Eugene, Oregon

stairs, clambering over tiles, giant concrete steps, cut blocks of red granite, and loose boulders into a checkered middle-level pool where it swirls around a concrete column and splashes off into a blue, ochre, and red tiled, rock-studded pool in the court below, provides a rustle of sound, shimmering surfaces, and an endless variety of flow patterns. It is, by Wingwall's own account, an imaginative replay of a canyon in the Ticino that she passed through once in a rainstorm. The Cascade, combined with the rock-embedded paving that Scott Wylie has laid in the floor of the courtyard, and the tower, stairs, bridges, and measured pace of your building's walls, makes this Geology Courtyard a place that is unusually intense and memorable.

Returning for a moment to Light that Plays, I can't resist relaying my most recent discovery. Bathing at midsummer midday in my outdoor shower at The Sea Ranch, I was suddenly embraced by a rainbow refracting from the shower's fine spray—Apollo's reward, you may say, for escaping the confines of the water closet.

• D E A R   D O N L Y N ,   I shouldn't omit the description of three other fountains, two of them my own, which, imperfect as they are, continue the attempt so splendidly mounted at the Trevi to connect water with the observer, to help it mean as much as it can to us. Gordon Cullen, writing in the *Architectural Review* thirty-five years ago, described the notion of "mental leaning-out-over" to describe the close contact with the water that makes it mean so much to us. He described the magical shore, that special sense one gets on a wooden dock of the water between the dock boards and all around, of one's having in some way passed the edge between the land and the domain of the sea. A modest fountain in a courtyard in a nunnery of Coimbra, Portugal, leads the visitor farther and farther into the realm of water. The fountain is a square basin with a walk from each side down a few steps and along a sunken way, with the water lapping at the edges to give the sensation of engulfment, then the steps lead up to a little circular island on which a single jet of water splashes. From the island four tiny bridges span to small enclosed chapels twice removed (through the water and over it) from the realities of the mainland ten feet away, but infinitely distant.

A fountain I worked on in Portland, Oregon, owes it greatest debt to the Trevi, I suppose. It wells from a basin that forms the back of a bench, so the seated visitors have a wall of water sliding down behind them. It then splashes and slides, froths, and plunges down a little canyon to a lower level where it flows between stepping stones to a reflecting basin intended at first to be a maelstrom out of Edgar Allan Poe, but perhaps fortunately now a placid lake. (Philip Johnson succeeded in making water disappear into the underworld in the Fort Worth Water Park. The effect is awesome but perhaps not really Portland.)

The strength (the modernity maybe) of our Lovejoy fountain is its construction: 5 1/2 inch concrete steps simply formed behind 2 x 6 boards. But for a long time that was its weakness too. The Trevi is modeled so that where the water flows the travertine is smooth, and where the water is not the travertine is rough, representing the stone or growing plants.

Fountain at Coimbra, Portugal

The Lovejoy is all concrete—great if it's raining, but unable on a sunny day to define a place for the water that splashes at random onto adjacent verticals. It is improving though, after twenty-five years, as green moss grows on everything.

A fountain ten years later was built to celebrate the Italian community in New Orleans. It started as an artifact for St. Joseph's Day, March 19, when the Italian community in New Orleans lays out giant altars of food (in a city enchanted by great food), which figures in ritual actions by a juvenile Jesus, Mary, and Joseph, and is given later in the day to the poor. Our fountain in the Piazza d'Italia is, of course, about water, but it had to be Italian was well: and what, we asked each other, was the most Italian image we could think of? Italy! So we had a striped circular fountain basin built with a 70 foot-long relief map of Italy useful (though it has never been used) for a St. Joseph's Day altar. Water splashes down the rivers—the Po, the Arno, and the Tiber—and I proposed tiki torches on Etna and Vesuvius, but that was rejected as tacky (water is beloved, fire tacky. . . .).

More water was required. What else was Italian? The Classical orders! (With a boost from the Greeks.) So we in vented colonnades of each of the five orders: Tuscan, Doric, Ionic, Corinthian, and Composite. Tuscan was simplest—a ring of water to make what was supposed to be an unfluted column, though the closely spaced jets begin to suggest fluting. The Doric got metopes of water jets and stainless steel columns split like an ancient helmet to reveal water running down inside and a stainless steel wall behind the columns with water running down the surface. In the corners above the central arch on the

Doric wall I had thought to put huge windshield wipers to push away the falling water, but that suggestion was rejected as tasteless, only to be replaced furtively by my head spouting water. The Ionic order had water flying around in volutes, a liquid egg and dart molding. The Corinthian sported capitals of acanthus-shaped jets, and the Composite combined those with volutes of water and jets up between the fluting. At the top of the Alps was to be a delicatessen of German derivation. In the center of the concentric stripes, which are distorted to form the Italian peninsula, the focal point and speaker's platform is on Sicily, from which 95 percent of the Italians in New Orleans have derived. Sardinia provides additional seating for the Sicilian speaker.

The top-most columns are outlined in neon, reminiscent for me of the most elegant neon in the world, in the arcades in Turin. The connection was stronger in local minds to the neon on some famous bars, and was therefore questioned. Nothing ventured, nothing gained.

In any case, the Trevi is still ahead in the "mental leaning-out-over" race.

Inspirations

14 Images that Motivate 283

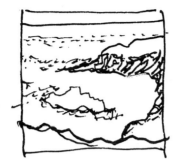

Two images that haunt us are geodes and chocolate sundaes. Geodes are magic stones: rough on the outside, but crystalline within, with sparkling facets around a tiny cavern that the imagination endows with breathtaking dimensions. It has been honored in Russian Easter eggs and in such buildings as the Alhambra in Granada—rough on the outside, crystalline on the inside. Geodes remind us that the inside of a building doesn't have to be at all like the outside, and that the littlest structure can shelter infinities of space and light. Chocolate sundaes suggest overspilling abundance.

●   DEAR DONLYN,   One Memory Chamber needs still to be considered: it's tempting to call it the Dream, but more properly modest to speak of Image. Images that Motivate. Architects, like most people, usually have some images they specially cherish: natural—like purple mountain majesties or amber waves of grain, or the breadth of the skies (in big sky country) or the mysteries of the forest; or maybe man-made—canyons of steel or the lights of home gleaming through the sycamores. Some architects have special images that give shape to what they would like to design. Le Corbusier had a powerful image of skyscrapers in a park, a vision he espoused so eloquently that whole cities came to be built that way. You and Bill Turnbull had, I thought, a wonderful image of a reef that you were going to shape of wrecked cars and sink offshore alongside the piece of

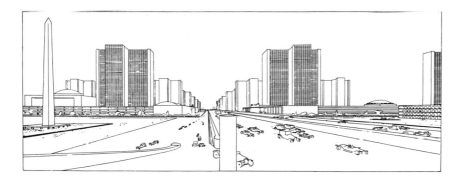

City of Tomorrow (Le Corbusier drawing, copyright Fondation Le Corbusier, used with permission)

San Francisco Embarcadero that you made into a concrete waterfront for relaxing. There was the prospect of underwater lights revealing, while they concealed, intimations of a fragment of a lost Atlantis.

I have an image I try sometimes to turn into buildings; you suggested it once, or rather gave form to it when you pointed out that my designing a building was like eating an ice-cream cone on a hot day, licking frenziedly on the drops that threaten to spill. That calls up an image of a building recollecting a chocolate or even hot fudge sundae: the image is a top-heavy one, of course, of roofs and chimneys and dormers and bays all bigger than the chaste and smaller base on which they tumble and slide. A very few Medieval buildings, especially in France, do this as they search upward for light. A seaside village, very compact, built in Malta as a movie set for Popeye, did it, though it is more like a banana split. But mostly the chocolate sundae is an image for the future: do not confuse it with mashed potatoes, which start the same, heaped to overflowing, but then are made centripetal, by a crater filled with gravy. The mashed potato image does not, I think, have the generosity or the potential for surprise that good architectural images require.

Another image that has for a long time been exciting for me is the geode. Geodes are magic stones, rough on the outside but with a crystalline cavern within, with sparkling facets around a tiny space that the imagination endows with breathtaking dimensions. The same magic is found within Russian Easter eggs and in a few buildings, especially the Alhambra in Granada—a rough stone fortress on the outside, with symmetrical gatherings of spaces inside around courtyards of delicate crys-

289

Geode diagram

talline complexity, some tiled, some made of thousands of plaster shards painted and bathed in light reflected from the surface of splashing fountains. A gentler geode image is found in canyons or narrow valleys. C. S. Lewis in *Out of the Silent Planet* imagined the inhospitable surface of Mars to be crossed with deep defiles that held enough oxygen to sustain life. Oak trees grow, like the Martians, in little canyons on the California grassy slopes where there is some extra surface water. The sculptor Charles Simon set miniature valleys into the mortar joints of urban walls, suggesting a scale of imagined landscapes within the much more familiarly scaled bricks and mortar of masonry walls. The power of miniatures plays a part here in concentrating our attention on a special inside (valley or court or mortar joint) very different from the vast bland outside, surprising even and satisfying as it helps give shape to our visions.

People love little things, from toy forts and doll houses to puppet theaters and bonsai, to miniature villages and electric trains. Probably their smallness makes us feel bigger than usual, and in better control. The dweller standardly seeks, like Goldilocks among her bears, a middle way, with surrounds neither too big nor too small, but just right. Sometimes, though, as for Alice or Gulliver, there is an advantage to scaling things up, or down, for a new look, a surprise, a convenience, maybe even an insight. Enlist me with Alice and Gulliver. There seems great potency in the world of little things, from Disneyland to miniature villages to toy trains. At Disneyland on Main Street the buildings around you are about seven-eighths full size, diminishing on the upper floors to something like five-eighths. The visitor therefore is bigger than usual, and in fuller control. The small surrounds aren't small enough to pinch, but are small enough to give the visitor the great comfort of feeling supernormally in charge.

Disneyland is exciting and close to full size. But some of the same feeling comes from much smaller settings into which we have to project ourselves. The most seductive I know are in Alexander Girard's Folk Museum in Santa Fe, assembled out of folk art from all over the world in cases large and small. In large cases are river banks lined with boats, and mountain of Hispanic and Indian and Victorian houses, and elegant drawing rooms, and Polish churches; small cases exhibit tinier treasures.

It's an exotic world, but mostly friendly or at least exciting, as in the bull ring or in devil-bestrewn hell.

Miniatures help lead us into the realm of architectural fairy tales: there needs to be such a genre. Bruno Bettelheim wrote a fascinating book, *The Uses of Enchantment,* describing the real need for fairy tales for children, to introduce them to evil in carefully measured doses that are real but surmountable; a kind of toxin antitoxin, not trivial or cute as they often become nowadays. Evil is serious, but not invincible. The young hero or heroine in a seesaw struggle can deal with it—and however long they are on their mission, they'll make it home in time for tea. I spent a springtime in Rome once looking for architectural fairy tales, and I found many: places, for instance, where the uncertain edge brushes up against the sheltered middle, as if a fresh breeze were blowing from a far off and mysterious place, as at the Aqua Paola where formal openings in the facade give directly onto wild gardens just behind. It's not evil that we are overcoming here, but mass—or the presence of solidity, maybe, as an expression of reality. This absence of mass can be taken as an equivalent of the absence of size the basis for images that unsettle and freshen our perceptions.

You, Donlyn, have pointed out that over the years I have depended increasingly on a design strategy that focuses on picking out a small part of each design to lavish attention on, relieving the rest of the design for more functional requirements. A case in point is the Howard Hughes biological laboratories at the University of California in San Diego, which is mostly laboratories carefully planned for light, filtered air, fume hoods, and turbulence of intertwining swirls, endlessly changing yet always roughly predictable. At low tide the turbulence would have increased, splashing around the forms of the reef, itself revealed as a repository of surprising sculpted elements, replete with pockets of still water and murky associations with the deep.

There is one difficulty, though, with your memory of the image—it was never intended to be made of wrecked autos. Now I will admit that they would have made shapes interesting enough for the water to curl around, and that they would have had the advantage of rusting, changing, and fusing over time, and that they might have lent a certain macabre charm to the image; but we intended to make the reef of concrete, with walls, steps, pools, and bronze and ceramic sculpture; items that would certainly become suitably layered with algae, but that would have the capacity still to capture moments of hopefulness.

It's curious that you should have remembered it in the likeness of wrecked cars; perhaps it fused in your memory with

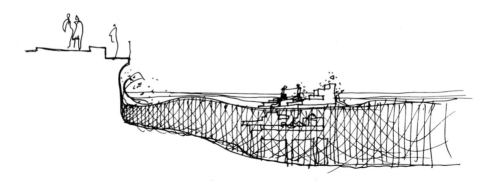

Reef proposal for Embarcadero, San Francisco, California

the junk sculptures in the Berkeley mud flats, then on the opposite side of the Bay, that I wrote about long ago, citing them as evidence of our generation's will to make some sort of free-verse sense out of the global situation into which we had, in the 1950s, been thrust. Now that our generation is at least partly responsible for the mess, free verse seems less hopeful, unfettered entrepreneurs appear as likely to destroy as to create, the romance with "collisions"—so beloved in current critical discourse—is far less compelling.

To suppose that our reef could ever have made the tidal lappings of the Bay become anything nearly as suggestive as the splendor of those surf-surrounded rocks outside the condo requires a considerable leap of faith. Yet it seems a suitable reason to return once again to the image—maybe dream *is* the better word—of creating places that have the qualities that characterize that surf-filled cove: deep history, exhilarating presence, fundamental lawfulness, cyclical change, sparkling light, and infinitely surprising detail. It's an image we've admired, in Chinese landscape paintings and in thousands of variants on the beach, in the forest, in vernacular cities, and in the finest monuments of the Baroque. And it's a dream worth pursuing in consort with nature and like-minded folk.

The Castello di Gargonza, Italy

Memories lodge in places that are distinct. Axes, orchards, platforms, boundaries, openings, canopies, and markers, when interwoven with our movements through them and the light that plays across them, set out an intricate web of relationships that can ensnare moments from our lives and hold them in safekeeping. Places, humble or grand, that become palaces for memory meld these themes into compositions, with rooms and spaces complexly ordered in patterns both familiar and mysterious, enlivened by ornament and association and intertwined with gardens, water, and evocative imagery.

• DEAR CHARLES, Returning to the Castello di Gargonza with our Memory Chambers in mind has been enlightening. My first reaction was to be surprised, again, at how small the place is. The second was to find, again, how full it is with the lessons we propose—acting, of course, in concert not solo. It is gratifying indeed to find that the themes we've described can also be found in a place of vernacular origin, confirming for me their fundamental strength.

Take, for instance, *Axes that Reach*. It would seem an unlikely lesson to find in a small Medieval castello. Yet there it is at the top of the hill, in the densest part of the organization—a charged, straight-arrow vista that dashes between the church and the front door of Casa Niccolina. The example is imperfect to be sure: the building walls on either side wander back and forth to create a crooked channel of space about 7 feet wide; the ground rises to a peak midway so that from either end the full floor of the path cannot be seen; the doors are not exactly centered on the path at either end. But there it is nonetheless; a charge drawn between two points, vibrating with energy. It creates, I would contend, a central organizing idea of the place, the reference line against which positions in the Castello are measured—to one side or the other of that axis. *Paths that Wander,* on the other hand, describes the principal ways through the Castello that follow the surrounding walls, descending in loops from the tower and its piazza. The purely mental but precise visual charge that reverberates along the axis between those two

The Castello di Gargonza, church entry

doors on the ridge is given even greater force by contrast with the way that movement through the place unfolds, shaped directly by the sloping ground, often carved into the rock itself, always made either of earth or cut stones.

The Castello is also an encyclopedia of *Platforms, Slopes,* and *Stairs,* none of them very dogmatic. Nowhere do you experience the abstraction of a surveyor's level. Terraces slope with the hill as in the pine plantation or the vineyards. Buildings rise in stories from the sloping ground, but each level is usually entered from a point close to the ground itself, and the outer walls, stone and brick rising from the rocks, give no obvious indication of the levels within. The only really flat places outside are in the two walled gardens that belong to the manor and the commons house. Here platforms of planting are separated from the common paths and slopes to create oases of sunny peacefulness and outlook—places of special repose, even in a sleepy village. These stepped terraces create areas with differences in outlook and enclosure that follow still, a step removed, the slope of the land.

Stairs, as we say, *Climb* and *Pause.* Most stairs in Castello di Gargonza are modest—up a few steps to a landing if they are outside; tight, steep, and twisted if they are inside. The

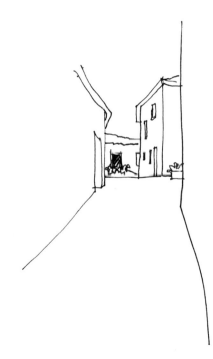

The Castello di Gargonza, Casa Niccolina

The Castello di Gargonza, entry ramp

The Castello di Gargonza, stairs and vista

most dramatic are two distinguished more by how they're made
than by how you move along them. One, which climbs up between buildings from the lower floor of the old olive press, is
in the vicinity of the quarry and is cut directly into the stone
with rough, irregular, but workable treads. Immediately adjacent
a ramped ledge offers a platform for urns of plants that provide
a colorful accompaniment to the climb. On the other side of
the same building is an entirely opposite condition: a long stone
stair reaches up without pause from the garden to an upper
room. It bridges across a small passage and is accompanied in its
upward thrust by grape vines on trellis sticks. These make a
lovely canopy of green that climbs out of the garden right up to
the door.

The same vine (and some mates descending) clambers down across the clay roofs of outbuildings and then across another wood trellis that crosses the lower path. The whole creates a shady, leafy transition between the two encircling paths that meet here at the lowest point in the compound bound together by the wall of the Castello and separated from the slopes below on either side. This lower area inside *Borders that Control* has the most complex *Walls that Layer* to be found at the Castello di Gargonza, with outbuildings of various widths, a fenced garden, a trellised recess, and another stair climbing high up to the building face. These create deep *Pockets that Offer Choice and Change* in the spaces to either side of a building mass that pro-

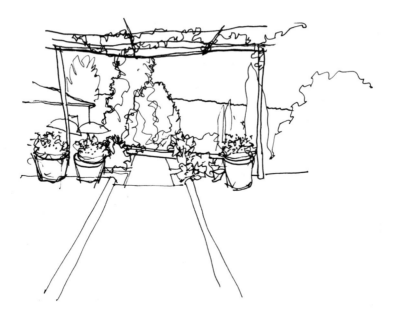

The Castello di Gargonza, commons garden

The Castello di Gargonza, paths

jects perpendicular to the other buildings and that once housed the communal oven. Here on the southeast side there is a large unpaved communal space between the wall and any buildings, no doubt a workyard once, now offering the greatest opportunity either for improvised activities or for change in the structure of the place.

Roofs Encompass clusters of buildings in the Castello, creating an endless variety of accommodating shapes as they adjust to the vagaries of curving walls, falling slopes, and improvised additions—all covered, of course, with the soft red tiles of

The Castello di Gargonza, well

Tuscany. Of *Canopies* there are none, save the umbrellas that *Center* visitors under their *Lulling Shade* in the garden of the commons building. *Light Plays* over all the nuanced stone surfaces of buildings and pavement, subtly shifting the grounds for perception as the day passes.

The Castello di Gargonza, insignia, Santa Maria della Scala

There's not a great deal of *Ornament* in the place, but what there is in the chapel *Transmits* the messages of the faith, *Transforms* this simple structure into a place of special interest and significance, and *Encodes* its role in the complex. Above the ornamented door of the manor house is a small curved ladder symbol that further encodes this structure as one of the outposts of Santa Maria della Scala in Siena, the powerful hospital opposite the cathedral that was once one of the major landholders in the region.

Water Pools, quietly, in a well underneath the plaza and *Connects* most visibly now from the spout of a faucet to one side of the entry road. For *Gardens that Civilize* we look to the axially divided and bordered gardens of the manor house on the one side, and to the loose *Orchard* of pine trees and the staked vineyards that set *Measure* to the walled gardens of the south.

309

As we've noted before, the tower of the Castello, with its *Shadow that Haunts* the streets of the village, is a storybook *Marker that Commands* the countryside—serving, in consort with elements from the rest of our Chambers, to etch this place in our memories.

The Castello di Gargonza is a repository for the recollection of pleasant thought-filled, sunny, and quiet days as well as a humble but handy Palace for the Mind—itself an *Image that Motivates*.

Boldface indicates illustrations.

319